SCHOOLS COUNCIL **WORKING PAPER 44**

Religious education in primary schools

Evans / Methuen Educational

First published 1972 for the Schools Council
by Evans Brothers Limited
Montague House, Russell Square, London WC1B 5BX
and Methuen Educational Limited
11 New Fetter Lane, London EC4P 4EE

Distributed in the US by Citation Press
Scholastic Magazines Inc., 54 West 44th Street
New York, NY 10036

© Schools Council Publications 1972

SBN 423 49640 9

Printed in Great Britain by
Richard Clay (The Chaucer Press) Ltd
Bungay, Suffolk

The team:

Clifford Jones – director
Carol Mumford }
John Conder. } field officers

Contents

Introduction

This report is an account of a survey of religious education in a number of primary schools in England and Wales. The schools are not a random sample: they were nominated because their religious education was considered by well-qualified observers to be above average in quality. It is therefore impossible to generalize with statistical confidence from our findings. Presumably we saw some of the best examples of religious education in the country, and we can only report, as objectively as possible, what we saw in the schools.

In addition to the survey we have attempted an assessment, made in the light of recent trends revealed in the literature of the last decade or so, of the work we saw in the schools. There is considerable evidence of a commendable desire on the part of many teachers and headteachers to keep abreast of modern thought on the subject of religious education, but the sad fact is that few of them have the necessary theological training to enable them to do so successfully. This unhappy state of affairs has prompted us to go beyond the strict limits of a survey and to offer certain suggestions that we consider to be in urgent need of being implemented, and we hope that these suggestions will be carefully considered by local education authorities and others responsible for the initial and the in-service training of teachers. In particular, we hope very much that teachers themselves will use this report as a basis for discussion, and that it will go some way towards solving at least some of their problems.

We do not pretend to know all the answers in this notoriously difficult area of the curriculum, nor do we think that there is anything strikingly new in our recommendations. Nevertheless, we believe that the difficulties in the situation offer a stirring challenge, and that the new knowledge at our disposal presents us with a splendid opportunity. We have not disguised these difficulties, nor have we shirked the task of setting out this new knowledge in a readable form. We are of the opinion that if the challenge is courageously accepted and the opportunity firmly grasped by the large number of sincere and devoted teachers working in primary schools today, the situation could be improved in a comparatively short time. We hope this report will stimulate discussion and encourage action in the field of primary-school religious education. It should be read alongside Working Paper 36, *Religious Education in Secondary Schools* (Evans/Methuen Educational, 1971) from the Schools Council Project on Religious Education in Secondary Schools at the University of Lancaster.

I. The programme

The project was launched at the Institute of Education, University of Leeds, in September 1969 with a part-time director, Clifford Jones, two full-time research officers, and some part-time secretarial help. It extended over eighteen months (excluding the writing of this report) and during that time the following programme was carried out.

i   A survey was made of the religious education in a nominated sample of 213 primary schools in England and Wales.
ii   Visits were made to a selected sub-sample of fifty-six schools. The survey and the visits covered the daily assembly, formal and informal religious education, moral education, community service, school relationships, and the integration of religious education with other school activities.
iii The opinions of a number of teachers and headteachers were obtained on various aspects of religious education.
iv   Recent literature and research in the field of religious education, especially as they apply to the primary school, were reviewed and critically evaluated.
v   Trends in primary-school religious education during the past decade were identified.

The project revealed a number of topics calling for further investigation, and it is hoped that these will be studied in a substantial development project to be initiated in the near future. We cannot stress too strongly the need for this second project to continue the work we have begun.*

* A three-year curriculum development project on religious education in primary schools will be established at the Department of Religious Studies, University of Lancaster, from May 1973, under the direction of Professor Ninian Smart.

II. Selecting the schools

First, nominators were approached and 110 of them agreed to serve. They represented local education authorities, HM Inspectorate, colleges of education, and the religious denominations. They nominated 304 schools, considered to be 'notable for the high quality of their religious education'.

Next, a questionnaire was prepared and subjected to pilot testing. Copies of the questionnaire in its final form (reproduced in Appendix A) were sent to the 304 nominated schools. Headteachers in 213 of these schools (representing 70 per cent of the total) returned completed questionnaires.

Finally, using the information in the questionnaires, a sub-sample of fifty-six schools was selected from the main sample of 213 schools. The selection procedure ensured that the sub-sample contained schools which are treating religious education seriously, and are ready to explore, or are already exploring, the new approaches to religious education. In addition, schools were included in the sub-sample which covered as wide a variety of different types as possible: large and small, country and urban, county and voluntary, schools with and without teachers specially qualified in religious studies, schools with a high proportion of immigrant children and schools with few or none, schools in which an experimental approach has been adopted and those in which a more formal attitude is maintained.

III. Planning the visits

A letter was sent to each of the headteachers of the fifty-six selected schools, asking for the following facilities to be made available for the visiting member of the project team:

a to be allowed to spend two whole days in the school;

b to be granted an interview of substantial duration with the headteacher at the beginning of the visit to enable the visitor to obtain a general view of the school and its work and to discuss the religious education in the school;

c to be allowed to share in at least one assembly;

d to be allowed to meet the staff as a group, apart from the headteacher, to discuss with them their approach to religious education;

e to be able for most of the time to move round the school, talking to individual teachers and children – it was made clear that we did not wish either assembly or teaching to be specially prepared or artificially introduced for our benefit, but that obviously we hoped to see some religious education in progress;

f to be shown examples of expressive work in religious education previously done by children;

g to be allowed to submit to the headteacher and the teachers a short questionnaire (see Appendix B).

In almost every case these facilities were freely granted, and we were made welcome and helped in every possible way. In only a very few cases were we rebuffed; occasionally we were lavishly entertained.

An agreed procedure for conducting the school visits was then evolved, and the three members of the project team visited five schools together to practise and standardize the procedure. They then visited the other 51 schools individually. One member of the team visited schools in Lancashire and Yorkshire; another visited schools in Wales, the western half of England and two Inner London Education Authority schools; and the third visited schools in the eastern half of England, one school in Wales, one in the north-west, and one ILEA school. The visits took place from April to October 1970, excluding August.

IV. Recent trends in religious education (Cm)

Radical changes have taken place during the last ten years in our thinking about the purpose of religious education in the primary school. To understand these changes it is necessary to look at them in the wider context of the general changes that have occurred in educational thought during the same period; changes in our ideas about the intellectual and emotional development of young children.

First, there has been a fundamental shift of emphasis from the subject-matter of instruction to the needs and capabilities of children. It is now believed that there are recognizable changes in the quality of children's thinking which take place in a regular sequence, and educationists no longer think that children progressively amass more and more knowledge and think about it more deeply as time goes on. This must obviously be taken into account in any consideration of the teaching material and methods that are appropriate for children at the various stages of their development.

Secondly, the significance of the emotional factor is now more clearly recognized. Whereas early intellectual achievement was formerly encouraged and regarded as being of prime importance, it is now realized that other aspects of growth must also be considered, and attempts are made to assess progress in qualities such as the ability to get on with people, to persevere with a chosen task, and to deal with frustrations. The aim of education is thought by some to be to help children to achieve all-round healthy growth of personality, and to reach the fullest possible stature at each stage of their development. Positive and creative attitudes nurtured at primary level are now seen to be of overwhelming importance for successful later learning.

Thirdly, there have been changes in our attitude to the curriculum. The advantages that come from children being strongly motivated and the concern that they shall acquire a working understanding of a range of ideas and principles have combined to make it less desirable for teachers to arrange their work in a restrictive or narrow way. Attempts are now made to help children to gain knowledge through their own experience, through the excitement of searching for truth, and through the joy of learning by finding out, as well as in more instructional ways. It is recognized that learning in one part of the curriculum may

8

be helped by learning in other parts, and the danger of the undesirable fragmentation of knowledge into separate subjects at this stage is reduced by having the timetable more broadly drawn.

Fourthly, there is a growing recognition that closer integration between the different sides of a child's experience makes for full and healthy growth, and that ideally this integration extends beyond the school to the homes and the neighbourhood in which children live.

The thinking and research that has brought about these changes in education generally, and in religious education particularly, must now be briefly reviewed.

1. The development of children's religious thinking

A fresh and deeper understanding of the thought processes and the learning abilities of children has been one of the important factors leading to the radical changes in primary schools in recent years. The effect of this new understanding upon the religious education of children and adolescents has been investigated by a small band of educationists, among whom Dr Ronald Goldman is the best known. This research has had a profound influence in the field of religious education and has given rise to a far-reaching reassessment of the place and purpose of the subject in the primary school.

Goldman's research was prompted by a general concern about the apparent ineffectiveness of the teaching based on the agreed syllabuses of religious education required by the 1944 Education Act. This concern was sharpened by the publication in 1961 of two books: *Teenage Religion* by H. Loukes (SCM Press) and *Religious Education in Secondary Schools*, a report from the University of Sheffield Institute of Education (Nelson). Both these books revealed widespread ignorance about the Bible and Christian belief among adolescents who had been given religious teaching throughout their school lives; and the nationwide application of the tests originally given only to children in Sheffield showed that this ignorance was by no means restricted to that city – see H. Loukes, *New Ground in Christian Education* (SCM Press, 1965), pp. 48–75. What was so amiss that many young people could go through ten years of compulsory religious education and at the end of it have little idea what religion was all about? Goldman decided to seek the answer to that question, and to give 'a descriptive account of how school pupils think about religion and the content of their thoughts as they are taught religion . . . so that teachers, parents, clergy, and all who are involved in religious education may see more clearly its problems and opportunities' (R. J. Goldman, *Religious Thinking from Childhood to Adolescence* (Routledge & Kegan Paul, 1964), p. xi). He took as a starting-point the conclusions reached by Jean Piaget about the stages of general concept development in young people and devised tests to discover whether similar stages can be discerned in religious concept development.

STAGES IN THE DEVELOPMENT OF CHILDREN'S GENERAL THINKING

Piaget observed three stages in the development of children's general thinking, corresponding approximately to the ages 4 to 7 years, 7 to 11 years, and from 11 years onwards. They may be described as the stages of intuitive thinking, concrete thinking, and abstract thinking. Two things need to be said about them. First, it must be stressed that although children pass through the intuitive and concrete stages before being able to engage in abstract thinking, they do so at different rates, and therefore the suggested age groupings may be misleading. Secondly, the same child may display different stages of intellectual development when faced with problems of different kinds. In the same way that an adult does not in one situation function at the level of which he is capable in another situation, so a child may respond differently according to the amount of experience he can bring to a situation or the extent to which he is interested in the problems it contains.

At the intuitive stage, thinking is fragmented and sometimes illogical. Young children tend to seize upon one aspect of a situation or a story – the one they can make sense of in terms of what is within their experience – and this then becomes of central importance to them, although to an adult it may be comparatively unimportant or even quite irrelevant.

Arrival at the concrete stage marks a breakthrough in thinking. The child now begins to be able to think more logically, to relate the different aspects of a situation, to classify data, and to check over his thinking. He is still limited, however, to thinking mainly about specific objects, and the ability to frame a hypothesis and to test it out is still beyond him.

The development of this latter ability marks the next great step forward into the stage of abstract thinking. At last the child is freed from the limitation to specific situations and objects, and he can now begin to think in abstract and symbolic terms, to formulate hypotheses and theories, and to trace and retrace the lines of thought in an argument, using both inductive and deductive reasoning in the process.

Using the Guttman scalogram method, Goldman analysed the responses to questions based on selected pictures and Bible stories and observed that children and adolescents pass through the same stages of development in their religious thinking as in their more general thinking, but that there is a delay in the onset of the stages in the case of religious thinking compared with general thinking. After warning his readers about the impropriety of suggesting specific age ranges for the various stages, he says that in religious thinking the mental ages corresponding to the stages of development are approximately up to 7 or 8 years for intuitive thinking, from 7 or 8 to 13 or 14 years for concrete thinking, and from 13 or 14 years onwards for abstract thinking. It must be emphasized that these are *mental*, not chronological ages.

Goldman inferred that children at the intuitive level tend to accept Bible stories at their face value and that they are unable to recognize analogies, for example about the nature of God, for what they are, and they therefore accept them as statements of fact. God is often regarded as a frightening, unpredictable person possessing magical powers, who can cast spells, punish, and pay back for misdemeanours. That God is a friend, though sometimes stated, seems to be only very partially grasped either intellectually or emotionally, and great confusion is evident about the God–Jesus relationship.

Even when children reach the concrete stage of thinking and are beginning to be able to reason more clearly, they are still hampered by literalism, seeking to make sense of Bible stories at their face value, and judging problems in terms that bear a relationship to what they know through their own limited experience. Inner meanings elude those who can only think in terms of the concrete, and who are still preoccupied with attempts to find physical explanations which meet the facts as they see them. Ideas about God at this stage are only a little less crude than those of younger children, and biblical material that is symbolic or in parable form will almost certainly be misunderstood. There is considerable evidence to show that children at this stage try to make sense of baffling material in terms of the simple everyday science with which they are now becoming familiar.

Only after reaching a mental age of 13 or 14 years do young people have the intellectual ability to consider an incident or a situation from the point of view of its underlying meaning, and to make the transferences needed to deal with symbolic expressions.

The slowness in religious concept development compared with concept development in other areas of thought revealed in Goldman's research had been noted twenty years earlier by Ernest Harms in his investigation of the development of religious experience in children. Feeling strongly that children's verbal expressions of their religious experience give only partial and inadequate information about their total religious life, he attempted a study of children's imaginative drawings and paintings and their comments about them. Like Goldman, he found three stages of development, which he described as the fairy tale, the realistic, and the individualistic stages, and he concluded that the 'entire religious development of the child has a much slower tempo than the development of any other field of his experience' ('The development of religious experience in children', *American Journal of Sociology*, Vol. 50, 1944, No. 2, pp. 112–22).

Goldman sums up the implications of his findings about the religious teaching of young children in this way: 'The greatest danger for the infant pupil is that of acquiring a religious vocabulary which has no conceptual substance, comparable to possessing a number vocabulary without number insights. For this reason and in the light of our evidence of gross distortion in terms of verbal misunderstanding, emphasis in infant schools (and in the first two years or more in junior schools) should be increasingly in terms of influence rather than instruction . . . Bible teaching as such would appear to be wasteful and inappropriate with these younger children' (*Religious Thinking from Childhood to Adolescence*, pp. 232 f.).

Goldman's research methods have been challenged and his findings have been questioned, but his general conclusions about religious concept development have been accepted by many educationists. His work in this field has been a powerful stimulus to radical thinking about religious education, and it has brought about fundamental changes in the outlook and the practice of those responsible for it, not least in the primary schools of this country.

2. The emotional development of children

A glance at the introductory articles in almost any of the recently revised syllabuses of religious education will show that the intellectual development of children is only one of the factors taken into account when religious teaching is being considered. Much is written about their personal needs for love, acceptance, and security; and religious education is seen in the context of total growth towards wholeness of personality. Teachers should therefore be aware of the emotional stresses which young children experience as they try to come to terms with an ever-widening society, and they should be perceptive enough to know when it is right to speak and when to be silent. Sympathetic understanding of the crude ideas children are likely to bring to early confrontation with the vocabulary of religion is another essential, if teachers are to help children to transform and refine their ideas. This is obviously a very different approach from the intellectual approach to child development.

R. S. Lee, in *Your Growing Child and Religion* (Penguin Books, 1965), discusses the psychological insights that are the foundations upon which this aspect of child development rests, and draws out what he considers to be its implications for spiritual growth. He argues that it is impossible to isolate religious development from the development of the whole personality, and says: 'Religion is much more a matter of what a man or woman is than what he believes or does. It is an attitude of mind and heart and will lie in the shape of the self, the personality, rather than in a set of doctrines and rules of conduct that are believed or followed. These latter can be taught; the other can only be fostered.' (p. 12)

The set of a child's life has already been established before he comes to school, and this will make it either easier or more difficult for him to establish trustful, warm relationships with other people and with God. In a home where there is love that does not seek to possess, where there is consistent treatment and wise protection, the pre-school child already has a basic security which enables him to face his world with confidence, to venture, to meet frustration and pain with courage. Within such a home a child can grow in awareness that, whatever his behaviour, he is loved for his own sake and not for any extraneous reason. His capacity to respond in such circumstances is enormous, and he can rejoice in doing things for those he loves and can begin to accept voluntarily a measure of self-discipline. In doing so he is moving away from a purely self-centred view of life, and religious development is already taking place.

A child who is denied this kind of home background and who must face frustrations greater than he has the capacity to bear, is already at risk and his future mental and spiritual health is threatened. He may retreat into a fantasy world, continually seeking to escape hardship rather than to overcome it, or he may become so divided in his personality that it becomes almost impossible for him to make a response of love to people or to believe in a God of love.

When the question is asked, 'Who is God?', the answer frequently given to young children is in terms of a 'loving father'. The way in which an adult thinks about this phrase will depend upon his mature experience of God, but although he experiences God as personal, an understanding believer does not make the mistake of thinking that God is a person. A human relationship has been used to express a conviction about his relationship to God. This presupposes the ability to transfer an image, and we saw earlier that a child under the age of about 13 years is rarely capable of this kind of thinking, so that in the case of a young child the phrase 'loving father' is interpreted literally, and – whatever image a child has of his father – an image shaped by his emotional needs rather than based on reality will be applied to God. At its best, this is splendid; but more often the child is less fortunate and his picture of God is compounded of the ideal father and the one who is sometimes angry, always unpredictable and often to be feared. Crude father-God images easily become fixed, and many an adult still has an infantile view of God with all its consequences in an impoverished spiritual life.

In view of all this it is considered by some educationists to be unwise to raise the subject of God with young children. Lee writes: 'The topic of God is fraught with risk for the young child's future development in his religious ideas and attitudes . . . no doctrinal or moralistic teaching should be forced upon the child. If he does not raise the topic of God, it should not be raised with him. Any religious teaching given in this period should be given only in answer to questions.' (p. 134)

In the past churches and schools assumed that young children could be trained in habits of worship, and instructed in religious belief and rules of conduct. The fear is that children's religious behaviour, often prompted by their willingness to please adults, was sometimes mistaken for religious understanding. Children *seemed* to understand what they were told, but all the time they were applying their own crude interpretations to it. Childish howlers, instead of amusing parents and teachers by their quaintness, ought to have startled them into a realization of what was happening, and they ought to have known that uncomprehending repetition is neither worship nor religion, and that it can be lastingly detrimental to both.

At last we are being made aware of our past mistakes. In the view of Lee and those who think like him, the aim to be kept in mind with children under about 13 years old is to encourage in them while they are still young an attitude of mind that will enable them to discover what religion is all about. Our efforts are bound to fail unless the total growth of the child is being nurtured and the personality is developing along the right lines. Lee's account, summarized above, of the religious development of children is written for 'all who are involved in the religious education of children, that is, parents, teachers, clergy, Sunday school teachers, and so on' (p. 7). It thus covers a wider field than we were asked to cover, and goes beyond what we believe to be the purpose of religious education in the county primary school (see below, pp. 58–9).

14

3. Religious education in recent literature on primary schools

Two reports on primary schools appeared in 1967, the only two on this subject to be published in recent years: *Children and their Primary Schools*: a Report of the Central Advisory Council for Education (England) (HMSO), known as the Plowden Report, and *Primary Education in Wales*, a Report of the Central Advisory Council for Education (Wales) (HMSO), known as the Gittins Report. Both had the same terms of reference: 'To consider primary education in all its aspects and the transition to secondary education.' As might be expected, the recommendations of the two advisory councils on many basic issues are similar, but in some areas (religious education is one of them) different conclusions were reached. In the Plowden Report a minority of the members of the Committee dissociate themselves from the main report, because they believe that religious education should not figure in the curriculum of the primary school.

THE PLOWDEN REPORT

In some ways the section on religious education in this report is unsatisfactory, but much honesty and realism have gone into the writing of it, and this makes it salutary reading for any who are willing to face the situation in the modern world and its implications for religious education in the primary schools of today. The failure of the members of the committee responsible for the report to reach final agreement on religious matters (there are two notes of reservation on religious education following to the main report) only serves to emphasize the difficulty of attempting to assess the place and purpose of religious education in the educational system in general and in primary schools in particular.

Discussing the general aims of education, the Plowden Report looks to the future and asks what our rapidly changing society will be like when the young children of today have grown up. Ought they to be educated to adapt themselves to society as it is now, or as it may become? In a time of transition such as ours, when the relative rights of society and of the individual are not clear, what agreement can be reached about objectives? What kind of adults will the future require? The report ventures to name the human qualities that will probably be of most value: adaptability in the face of rapid change, teachability so that new skills may be acquired as they become necessary, discrimination and the ability to withstand mass pressures, an inner balance that is dominated by neither intellect nor emotion, compassion that respects the opinions of others and enters with sympathy into their feelings, and an awareness of the obligation all men have to the community in which they live. (paras 493–5)

15

In encouraging the growth of these qualities, education must concern itself with 'the moral and religious development of the child' (para. 497), and recognize that 'a school is not merely a teaching shop, it must transmit values and attitudes.' (para. 505)

The report recognizes that these values and attitudes cannot be effectively transmitted if the schools work in isolation. The healthy development of the whole child, his physical, mental, emotional, and spiritual growth, requires the closest possible co-operation between home and school. Education in the future may need to include help for parents as well as for children, and the function of the school in society may change dramatically. If this happens a clarification of basic aims will become essential, for if parents and teachers are to work more closely together for the benefit of the children, they must be clearly aware of their common objectives. (paras 107–10, 113–18)

The sections of the report dealing specifically with religious education (paras 558–77 and pp. 489–93) reveal the confusion that exists among educationists in this field.

The first note of reservation signed by six members of the committee (pp. 489–93) tends to assume that religion is something that can be taught in intellectual terms. Religious education, it says, necessarily includes theology, an academic discipline which is 'too recondite and too controversial to be suitable for inclusion in the curriculum of primary schools' (p. 489). Children should not grow up 'in ignorance of the content of Christian beliefs' (p. 490), but the teaching about belief should come later, in the secondary school, when pupils are able to consider different points of view. Clearly, this is a purely intellectual approach to religious education.

The majority report sees things in a very different light (paras 558–77). Religion is more than cognitive. An act of worship can be 'a unifying force for the school' and 'in it children should find, in brief moments, a religious expression of their life in school' (para. 570). Religion can 'illuminate personal relationships' (para. 571), and children 'may appreciate poetically what they cannot grasp intellectually' (para. 573). Clearly, this is *not* a purely intellectual approach to religious education.

THE GITTINS REPORT

Religious education is seen in the Gittins Report not simply as teaching 'a series of historical facts', but rather as the transmitting of 'a way of life which affects actions and relationships and determines attitudes', and it is suggested that children are most likely to be influenced by teachers who have faith as well

16

as professional skill (para. 20. 2). It is accepted that 'experience is the only effective basis for the development of concepts', and that teachers should follow the example of Jesus who 'never taught "religion", but taught about life and compelled men and women to look into the depths of their experiences and find in them a fuller meaning' (para. 20. 4). Religion is not something outside ordinary experience, and in the school context it must not be isolated from other activities, but should come within the interrelated subject approach of the modern primary-school curriculum.

All this seems to reflect an awareness that enrichment of experience *in itself* has a significance for spiritual growth, and that it is perhaps the most effective influence in nurturing this growth. But the report also expresses views which give a different slant from this. Current trends in primary education must influence what is done in religious education, but 'certain limitations must be noted. Because of the nature of the subject, which differs from all others, the aim is different.' The aim is stated. It is 'to build up attitudes and relationships: Christian attitudes to God, to people, to prayer, that will ultimately make religion the guiding force in pupils' lives' (para. 20. 4). It is clear, therefore, that what is advocated is teaching to establish Christian belief.

AMBIVALENCE IN THE REPORTS

It can be seen that both the Plowden and the Gittins Reports pay lip-service to the acceptance of the findings of psychology about the limitation in the thinking of young children, but that neither of them wholeheartedly accepts the implications of these findings for the practice of religious education. Neither report seems able to resist the compulsion of tradition. Whether or not they misinterpret them, children must be given the words of religion. Our task is to find more effective ways of communicating them. The point that children's misunderstanding of religious teaching may permanently hinder their religious development is not really taken in these reports. It is still a question of what adults think it is good for children to be taught. Stress is put upon trying to make children religious, and not enough consideration is given to the extent to which wrongly conceived religious education may spoil their appreciation of the nature of religion.

In spite of this criticism, both these reports are valuable in what they say about religious education, in that they draw attention to matters that urgently need further investigation. They make clear, for example, that before it can be decided what is *good* religious education, fundamental consideration must be given to the basic question, What is *religious* education? Furthermore, they drive us to make

17

an honest attempt to face certain questions that are of prime importance for the future of religious education: can religious education be integrated into primary-school work without making nonsense of the withdrawal clauses in the 1944 Education Act? Is the idea of having an agreed syllabus compatible with the modern approach to religious education in the primary school? What form should an act of worship for young children take? How far can religious education be incorporated in the general work of the primary school when teachers vary so considerably in their theological opinions, or when there is an absence of clearly thought-out or strongly held views?

AMBIVALENCE IN RECENT LITERATURE ON RELIGIOUS EDUCATION

The pull seen in the Plowden and the Gittins Reports between the recognition of what is educationally desirable and the concern to give children Christian teaching is also apparent in the recent literature on religious education. There is general agreement among writers of the past ten years that using the Bible as a book of moral instruction and indoctrinating children with religion are no longer educationally valid. It is, however, much easier to be negative than to say what should be done.

As early as 1961 Loukes, in his *Teenage Religion* (SCM Press), was urging teachers to recognize that religious education must increasingly be seen in terms of enlarging personal horizons, stimulating inquiry, and leading pupils towards an awareness of a deeper meaning in life. Loukes did not see this as excluding Bible teaching and Christian instruction, and he believed that a consideration of the Christian view of man is educationally valid within the context of the wider search for meaning. There should, however, be no attempt to indoctrinate. Religious education should rather be part of the whole broadening process of learning from experience. It should be seen as a quest for truth in which the religious view of life is set alongside other views, in which there can be no question of compelling pupils to subscribe to a set line, but in which they are helped to make informed judgements.

In his later book, *New Ground in Christian Education* (SCM Press, 1965), Loukes still holds that this is the most acceptable approach in the contemporary situation. Religious teaching cannot hope to be the same in a secular as it is in a religious society. In the present climate of religious uncertainty and rethinking, the 'authoritative transmission of a received tradition must give way to the open search for living truth; the hope of "making children Christians" must yield to a hope of opening young eyes to look for themselves.' (p. 175)

This is a very different emphasis from that found in Goldman's *Readiness for*

Religion (Routledge & Kegan Paul), also published in 1965. Goldman clearly believes that the way to make Christian teaching more effective is to devise more enlightened lesson content and better teaching methods. The ulterior motive of producing good citizens is condemned; 'Christianity should be taught because it is true, because it answers the deepest needs of human nature, and without a knowledge of the love of God and a relationship with him men and women will live impoverished lives' (p. 59). While at every stage working within the child's capacity to understand, Goldman would 'lead children to integrate all they are learning and doing in all subjects within a world view of God as creator and as the person who cares about his people.' (p. 197)

Edwin Cox's appraisal of the situation in *Changing Aims in Religious Education* (Routledge & Kegan Paul, 1966), contains elements of both these views. In formulating objectives he seeks to break away from the conventional aims of the older and immediately post-war agreed syllabuses, and looks for a starting-point in the needs of older pupils and adults. These he sees as the need to rediscover God in human experience and to deepen understanding of the nature of the Bible and of religious language, so that traditional symbolic statements can be seen for what they really are. In such a context religious education would seek to lead older pupils to ask basic questions about human existence, helping them to understand some of the answers men have found satisfying in the past. It would try to ensure that 'the school leaver has sufficient knowledge to make a serious and an informed judgement about religion' (p. 84). To be able to establish genuine open-endedness at this later stage, primary-school education should nurture attitudes which make possible an understanding of and a favourable attitude towards a religious interpretation of life, and it should refrain from whatever might inhibit later critical thinking or interest in religious issues.

Clearly, Cox envisages the use of modern approaches to religious education to make possible a religious understanding of life, and his specific suggestions indicate Christian values as the frame of reference in dealing with personal relationships. (p. 87)

A more recent and a thought-provoking contribution to the search for a positive way forward is J. W. D. Smith's *Religious Education in a Secular Setting* (SCM Press, 1969). In this he surveys the present situation and demonstrates the impossibility of giving genuine Christian education in a secular society.

Older agreed syllabuses, he reminds us, assumed that Christian principles should influence the whole of education and mould attitudes to life. A quotation from the 1947 London Agreed Syllabus reflects the spirit of many others when it asserts that 'the ultimate aim of religious education is not to get over to the children a body of facts, but to inculcate and foster a comprehensible way of

19

life. This way of life is summed up in the words of our Lord, "Thou shalt love the Lord thy God . . . and thy neighbour as thyself." ' Smith contends that these words only make sense in the context of a believing society. Christian education is no longer viable in state schools, and even voluntary schools are facing problems arising from the unavoidable tensions between contemporary culture and the traditional teaching of Christianity. It is unrealistic to maintain any longer that Christianity can be the cohesive force giving unity of purpose to the whole school curriculum. 'Genuine Christian education awaits the emergence of a Christian community, renewed and unified in thought and life.' (p. 68)

How then does he visualize religious education today? Certainly as much more than simply that which enriches experience and fosters all-round development. It is not just 'learning for living'. He sees it rather as 'learning for life and death', facing the inescapable religious dimension in human experience, leading pupils to the 'frontiers of mystery', to the ultimate concerns of human existence. He stresses the need for Christian and non-Christian educators to come together to explore the educational function of religious education in state schools, starting perhaps from 'a recollection of our common humanity' and 'the mystery that confronts us all'.

This is a powerful plea that the ground of religious education should be shifted from the traditional, but no longer acceptable, transmission of the teaching of a particular faith to a more philosophical open approach, but in the last resort the reader is still left uncertain about what is really intended, for Smith concludes: 'If we can awaken our pupils to an awareness of mystery we shall have begun to fulfil the appropriate purpose of religious education in a state school curriculum . . . We shall fulfil the aims appropriate to religious education in the state schools of today and tomorrow if we deepen our pupils' insight into the Christian symbols of the cross and the empty tomb . . . the Christian interpretation of the mystery at the frontiers of human experience.' (p. 113)

The Durham Report, *The Fourth R* (National Society and SPCK, 1970), leaves no room for doubt in its intention. Clearly, it holds that whatever is done in the name of religious education must be educationally sound, and whatever Christian teaching is given must be set within the whole broadening educational process. Religious education is seen as part of an exploration into 'the place and significance of religion in human life', thus making 'a distinctive contribution to each pupil's search for a faith by which to live' (para. 215). The teacher's task is to encourage the understanding of Christian insights into fundamental questions of human existence, into personal relationships, and to consider what views are held by other religions and belief systems where this seems appropriate and helpful. The teacher must seek 'to initiate his pupils into knowledge which he encourages them to explore and appreciate' rather than into 'a system of belief which he requires them to accept' (para. 216). The conviction is clearly stated, however, that in this country 'the content of the curriculum . . . should consist mainly of the exploration of the literature and beliefs of the Christian faith.' (para. 214)

So far in this summary the question of whether religious education has a valid place in the school curriculum has not been raised. What has been under discussion is the kind of religious education which is appropriate in the contemporary situation. Increasingly it is being insisted that whatever form religious education takes it must be educationally valid and capable of being justified on educational grounds. Indoctrination into a particular set of beliefs is no longer acceptable, and religious education on such a narrowly conceived basis is held to be both undesirable and inappropriate in state schools today. Pupils should be led to an awareness of the different lines along which man pursues his search for meaning in life, to the recognition and acceptance of responsibility for thinking through what is important in life, in relationships and in the use of natural resources. They must be helped not only towards the ability to make informed decisions but also to the translating of decision into action.

4. The relationship between moral and religious education

The question now arises as to how far, if at all, the approach described above is specifically religious. Can it not be seen as simply moral training and, if this is so, is religious underpinning necessary? Certainly in the past religion has been widely used to bolster morality, not always by appealing to man's intellectual faculties but often by working upon his fear of consequences or by manipulating his emotions. The compilers of the older agreed syllabuses hoped that religious teaching would produce good citizens whose behaviour would be governed by Christian ethical standards. In the current theological turmoil it is no longer easy to be so sure about what Christian commitment requires, and traditional answers are no longer accepted without question. Not surprisingly, therefore, some are arguing that the real need in schools is for good moral teaching, and there is much discussion about the relationship between moral and religious education. Several lines of approach are reflected in recent publications.

The Farmington Trust Research Unit, directed by John Wilson, was set up in 1965. It is working on a long-term project to consider all aspects of moral education, and one reason for establishing the unit was the feeling 'now widely shared' that religious education alone cannot provide 'a completely satisfactory framework for moral education'. The reason for saying this is stated as the fact

21

that our society includes 'people of many religious creeds and of none', while those who believe cannot agree either about the interpretation of their own beliefs or the place they should have in religious education (J. Wilson, N. Williams, and B. Sugarman, *Introduction to Moral Education* (Penguin Books, 1967), p. 177). This first publication from the Farmington Trust seeks to clarify the nature of moral education by bringing together philosophical, psychological, and sociological points of view, and in so doing it challenges the assumption that morality is necessarily dependent on religion.

Another group of people grappling with the relationship between moral and religious education is the working party set up by the Social Morality Council. Their report, *Moral and Religious Education in County Schools* (Social Morality Council, 1970), is based on three years of study and discussion by this working party, which includes both believers and non-believers. It encourages 'men and women of all faiths and of none to find common ground from which to face the vast moral issues of our time: world poverty, international peace, race relations, control of environment'. In the face of a multiplicity of moral traditions, as diverse as the many religious faiths of mankind, where is a starting-point to be found? The report points to the interdependence that is fundamental to human existence and holds that through the ages broad areas of moral agreement are more impressive than those of disagreement. Perhaps along these lines some common foundations may be discovered. Morality is not thought of as depending upon a particular religious outlook, and moral and religious education are not regarded as identifiable with each other.

Religious education is recognized in the Social Morality Council report as study leading to an understanding of what religion is about, and an approach to religious education is envisaged which 'makes comparisons and requires judgements to be justified', in which pupils learn 'to distinguish superstition, religious custom, and reasonable faith, whilst gaining information about, and insight into, the beliefs and practices studied.' (p. 9)

Religious education seen from this point of view, as education into the understanding of the religious element in human experience, can properly be regarded as educational. Moreover, there can be no question of religious education being simply a means to moral education. The Durham Report also makes this point in its section on moral and religious education (Chapter 3). There it is pointed out that whereas the 1944 Education Act assumed that Christianity would continue to be sufficiently typical of the majority of people in our society to allow it to be the main basis of moral education, this is no longer a tenable view. In the present situation it would be a mistake to continue to base moral teaching entirely on a religious foundation, since young people who reject organized religion may then also reject the moral standards associated with it. While religious education must necessarily include the moral implications of religious belief, and moral education must face the basic questions about human existence with which religion is concerned, both must seek to encourage personal responsibility for choice and action rather than to inculcate an unthinking acceptance of authoritarian views.

The Schools Council Moral Education Curriculum Project represents another line of approach. Although it is concerned with pupils of secondary-school age, it is not inappropriate to mention it here; first, because the experimental material devised by the project team under the title *In Other People's Shoes* has been extensively used in a modified form in primary schools, and secondly, because it is hoped that the work of the project will be extended to the primary-school age range in due course.*

The stated aim of the project is to help children 'to adopt patterns of behaviour which take other people's needs, interests, and feelings into account as well as their own', and the curriculum produced as a result of the project has been tested in two hundred schools. Discussion, role-play, partly-scripted dramatization and imaginative writing are among the methods used, and dogmatic teaching is scrupulously avoided. The aim of helping children 'to adopt a considerate style of life' was deliberately chosen because it seemed to be the one least likely to alienate adherents of any of the major world religions or the followers of any important school of morality.

About 70 per cent of 15-year-old pupils say they would welcome help from their schools with their moral problems, and this is taken to justify the production of a programme of moral education that attempts to give that kind of help. The curriculum material, under the title *Lifeline*, is published by Longman.

---

* A four-year curriculum development project to produce materials to assist in the teaching of moral education to pupils between the ages of 8 and 13 was established at St Hughes Hall, Cambridge, in September 1972, under the direction of Peter McPhail.

V. The survey

1. Headteachers' and teachers' opinions   (Cus), Cus.)

The information summarized below was gathered from three main sources:
the questionnaires (see Appendix A) completed by the headteachers of 213
nominated schools; the questionnaires (see Appendix B) completed by the
headteachers and teachers of the 56 schools visited; and the interviews with
headteachers, and with teachers individually and in staff groups. The information
provided by teachers and headteachers is reported as objectively as possible.
Our more subjective comments on it are to be found elsewhere (pp. 48ff).

THE AIMS OF RELIGIOUS EDUCATION IN THE PRIMARY SCHOOL

When the apparently simple question is asked: What are the aims of religious
education in the primary school?, it receives a bewildering variety of replies – as
we discovered when we put this question to primary-school teachers and headteachers. Some teachers admitted that they were unable to state their aims, and
these included both young teachers uncertain about their own religious beliefs
and older teachers who feel insecure in the present educational situation. Some
of the latter group are convinced practising Christians of long standing with
considerable experience of teaching religion in school, but they are no longer
sure of themselves; they are uneasy about teaching the Bible, and they now find
religious education an embarrassing subject. Such teachers are obviously in need
of help (see below, p. 70).

The task of classifying the large number of answers to the question about
the aims of religious education in the primary school is a daunting, but not an
impossible one. The replies fall into three groups, corresponding to the following
aims suggested by headteachers and teachers:

> First, to provide children with opportunities of enjoying religious
> experiences.
> Secondly, to give children a knowledge of the Bible.
> Thirdly, to help children to translate their learning about religion into life.

A little must now be said, mainly in anecdotal form, about the way in which
headteachers and teachers think about each of these aims.

24

The headmistress of a county infant school expressed the first aim when she said that she tried to provide in her school 'an attractive and challenging environment with an atmosphere of serenity which will give the child the same sense of security as is found in a good home'. Spiritual growth is likely to be fostered in a school where children are loved, cared for, understood, valued, and accepted for what they are, where standards are consistent, and where there is a feeling of homeliness. In such an environment, sensitivity to the needs of others is likely to develop and this will give the school community a sense of purpose, unity, and cohesion.

Some teachers deliberately go further than this. They say that they try to create an awareness of a loving Father who cares for all his children, while others seek to foster elements of awe and wonder in the child's experience by encouraging appreciation of the beauty, grandeur, and infinite variety in nature, recognized as God's creation. Joy in music, movement, colour, and pattern sometimes leads to moments of wonder which some teachers link to an experience of the presence of God. Some headteachers are of the opinion that the religious conviction of the teacher is a vital influence in creating the kind of atmosphere in which children can grow spiritually.

Difficult to describe in words, this aim is nevertheless considered by many teachers to be especially valuable in infant schools, where 'religious education' is probably too grandiose an expression to describe what goes on, and where 'spiritual growth' is the more appropriate expression.

Some teachers try to give children a knowledge of the Bible, because they believe that it is the main source of knowledge about religion. Few headteachers think that Old Testament stories should be extensively used in the primary school, or consider that biblical knowedge is a part of our cultural heritage that must be transmitted from one generation to the next. Nevertheless, it is accepted that children at school ought to be familiarized with the better known stories in the Bible, some adding that children of today are unlikely to hear these stories elsewhere and that they would be the poorer for not knowing them. Others regard the Bible as a source-book of moral education and they teach it for that reason if for no other.

Growing spiritually and gaining knowledge are not mutually exclusive, and they can happily go on side by side in the right kind of school atmosphere. The environment that nurtures the one is likely to encourage the other also. Those factors in a school which contribute to the sense of serenity and security should also stimulate children to explore, observe, question, judge, evaluate, and test for themselves, and many teachers believe that this kind of activity enriches children's experience and may heighten their awareness of the reality of God.

25

The third aspect of religious education, translating learning about religion into life, is frequently recognized, and teachers describe it in various ways. For example, they say that religious education should help children 'to find the real meaning of life and their place in God's scheme'; 'to find a religious view of the whole of life and experience'; 'to grow into whole people, able to understand themselves', etc.

Teachers and headteachers in voluntary schools agree that these three aims, as far as they go, are appropriate in church schools also, and when groups of teachers discuss religious education, those working in voluntary schools speak for much of the time in precisely the same language as their colleagues who work in county schools. Apart from the name of the school, it would, in many cases, have been difficult from the responses to the questionnaires to distinguish voluntary from county schools. Some headteachers in voluntary schools, however, while assenting to the three aims mentioned above, would not agree that they are sufficient to describe completely what they attempt to do in their schools, and it is in the additions they wish to make that the differences they see between voluntary and county schools are revealed.

Roman Catholic schools, in particular, aim to prepare children for their confirmation, first communion, and first confession while they are still in the primary school, and mass is regularly said not only in the local church but also in the school, with children taking a full part in the ceremony. The much later reception of young people into church membership in the other denominations means that aided primary schools do not function in quite this way in other than Roman Catholic circles, but the strong link with one local church is often a distinctive feature in aided schools, a link which would, of course, be quite improper in a county school.

The number of positive assertions in the questionnaires about the place of church schools in the educational system was surprisingly small. Some heads of voluntary schools express themselves forcibly in saying what, in their opinion, church schools ought *not* to do: 'Church dogma should be avoided'; 'Church doctrine never enters into the teaching here'; 'We are not expected to convert or to provide choir boys'; 'It is not the purpose of the church to fill pews', etc. On the subject of aims, as in so many other matters in religious education, there is clearly a wide range of opinions among teachers and headteachers.

THE QUALITY OF TEACHERS

Almost half the headteachers who completed the questionnaire made reference to the quality of teachers as an important factor in education, including religious

26

education, and many of them considered this to be the crucial factor. Quality is variously defined, but a fairly clear picture emerges from this wide expression of views. Schools require teachers who have a genuine concern to meet the needs of children; who set a good example by their behaviour in their dealings with children, parents, and other members of staff; who are relaxed, friendly, and out-reaching; who naturally and happily enter into the various experiences of children; and who are prepared to give freely of their time. Many headteachers believe that the great need is for teachers who understand what it is they are trying to do in their work in school; who have an easy control of children; who are well informed in a wide range of subjects; and who have the perception to see, and the enthusiasm to grasp, teaching opportunities when they arise.

THE RELIGIOUS BELIEF OF TEACHERS

Headteachers are divided in their views about how far Christian commitment is necessary for teachers engaged in religious education. A few, all of them heads of church schools, feel the need for a staff consisting of dedicated Christians. Some of them claim that it is difficult, perhaps impossible, to ensure that the entire curriculum is permeated by a Christian spirit if some of the teachers are agnostics or humanists. Other headteachers believe that a body of men and women of good will, whether they are people of strong religious faith or of none, working and planning together in genuine concern for the needs of children, can have an incalculable influence for good and can lay sound foundations for later religious learning.

Some headteachers who have attempted to assess more specifically the influence of belief on religious teaching made a point which is significant in view of the current enthusiasm for thematic teaching. One of them pointed out that the Inner London Education Authority agreed syllabus, *Learning for Life* (1968), says that 'the teacher's business is to grasp the opportunities that arise and develop them to the point where their religious significance is revealed' (p. 32), and suggested that teachers lacking religious conviction are not able to do this. Another headteacher put it this way: 'Many young teachers cannot make the link in themes and integrated schemes because they have no religious background themselves – it is a gap in their own lives.'

It was frequently said by headteachers that if Christian values are to have a place in the life of a school and if the teaching is to be in any significant sense religious, teachers themselves must be convinced that religion has a relevance to everyday life. The comments of two headteachers sum up this point of view: 'The greatest blessing is an able staff, all of them sympathetic towards spiritual

27

things'; 'The ideal situation in the primary school is that in which conviction is allied to a professional capacity to involve children in experiences which can be recognized as having religious relevance.'

The questionnaire submitted to teachers and headteachers asked for an indication of their religious beliefs, and it is at once clear that there is enormous variety in this respect (see Table 4, p. 77). Some teachers are frankly nonreligious and think that religion is irrelevant to modern life. They believe that certain aspects of religious education have no place in a state school. Where teachers have contracted out of attendance at assembly, for example, it is often on the grounds that they do not feel able to encourage children to pray to God when they themselves do not believe that he exists. The general view of one staff-meeting where two-thirds of the teachers were in their early twenties was that specifically Christian teaching contributes nothing of value to education. To meet a staff so nearly unanimous in this view was rare, but significant when it is remembered that this school, like all the schools in the sample, was nominated as a school notable for the good quality of its religious education.

Among young teachers in particular, there are many who are uncertain about their beliefs. Some are not interested in thinking further about religion; others are aware of their own confusion, but are at a loss to know how to resolve it. In some cases these teachers were educated in church schools and denominational colleges of education, and a few even said that they had been shaken into unbelief by their college course.

The distribution of belief among the staffs of the primary schools visited, set out in Table 4, p. 77, is as follows.

In the county schools 2 per cent of the teachers declared themselves to be atheists, 7 per cent agnostics, 17 per cent humanists, 31 per cent nominal Christians, and 43 per cent committed Christians.

In the voluntary Catholic schools there were no atheists, agnostics or humanists, 5 per cent of the teachers and headteachers said they were nominal Christians, and 95 per cent that they were committed Christians.

In the other voluntary schools there were no atheists, 3 per cent of the teachers said they were agnostics, 10 per cent humanists, 25 per cent nominal Christians, and 62 per cent committed Christians.

Ninety-four per cent of the total number of headteachers in all the schools said they were committed Christians, and the rest said they were nominal Christians. (The percentages given here are to the nearest whole number.)

One of the most controversial issues in the field of religious education today is concerned with the question, What is religious? and, as a direct consequence, with the further question, What is religious education? Some teachers confidently assert that because religion is about God, Jesus, the Holy Spirit, the Church, etc., religious education must deal faithfully with these subjects and that it therefore can be confined to the box labelled 'Religious instruction' on the school timetable. Others believe that it ought not to be restricted in this way, but that it should be concerned, as a member of the consultative committee of this project wrote, 'With the relationships and quality of life within the school and the community . . . the place of competition and punishment in the school, the organization of groups, the goals set before children, the use of authority and the sharing of responsibilities.' What *is* religious? It is obviously of considerable importance to know how teachers and headteachers working in schools nominated because they were considered to be 'notable for the high quality of their religious education' are thinking about this question, and their opinions are set out below.

When asked directly how they would define religious education in the primary school some teachers answered the question by lapsing into vague generalities, such as 'It's in everything we do'; 'It's a way of life'; 'It can't be discussed as an isolated subject.' Some were only slightly more specific, saying that religious education is moral training and relationship building, coming to terms with one's own abilities and limitations, having a reverence for life, growth in self-knowledge, etc. Others introduced a specifically theological note into their answers, defining religious education as the conscious linking of the wonder and beauty of the world, and delight in pleasurable shared experiences, with the existence of an all-creating and sustaining God. Among this group there are those who think that it is only this kind of belief in God that distinguishes religious education from moral education. Many teachers, and most headteachers, dismissed the question by saying, 'We use the thematic approach.'

Most of those who describe themselves as humanists, atheists, or agnostics seem to think that religious education taught by the thematic method is so watered down and so largely concerned with secular subjects that even they can teach it in this form without embarrassment. One of them said, 'I can do this with a clear conscience,' and another wrote, 'I can use this method without perjuring myself.' For a large number of teachers, and this group includes Christians as well as unbelievers and doubters, the thematic method means training children in moral principles based on the Christian ethic, and little else. Most of

29

these teachers see no need for specific Christian teaching in support of moral training. The teachers in this group who declare themselves to be Christians and who fall back on this view of thematic teaching do so for a variety of reasons: some because they are not sure what is the most suitable kind of religious teaching for children in the primary school; others because they recognize that their own knowledge of the Bible and of theological concepts is inadequate; and still others because it is their sincere conviction that moral education is the soundest possible basis for the later understanding of more definitely religious education.

Some teachers are profoundly disturbed by the introduction of thematic teaching in religious education. They see it as an abdication of the responsibility they think is imposed on teachers by the 1944 Education Act to give 'religious instruction . . . in every county school and in every voluntary school'. Their comments reflect their opinions: 'Religious education must be more than just about caring and good relationships'; 'The Goldman life-theme booklets just don't contain enough of the Bible or religion'; 'It takes too long to get to the religious part.'

It is clear that these teachers have accepted the view that thematic teaching means a secular theme developed at length, leading to a smattering of religion which is tacked on at the end of the exercise. They would consider that if the end were omitted no religious learning would have taken place.

Many headteachers who are attempting to create in their schools a challenging environment of the kind described above (p. 25) speak most appreciatively of teachers of all shades of religious belief and of none, who use life-themes in their teaching of religious education. The head of a large junior school, where fewer than half the teachers claim to be Christians, spoke with considerable warmth of his staff, some of them gifted teachers, skilled professional men and women, making a highly significant contribution towards the possibility of achieving his aim. In their attitude to each other and their genuine concern for children they are all helping to build a caring community in which standards of behaviour are being established, based on the conviction that individuals are to be respected as persons. In an area where there is little beauty, security, moral consistency, or love in the homes of many of the children, the staff of this school regard community building as their most important objective. The headteacher describes it as 'giving deprived children an experience of Christian love in community', and for him this *is* religious education. Some of his staff regard it as 'giving children from immoral or amoral homes experience of values based on respect for people', and for them this is *not* religious education.

On the subject of statutory religious education there is a definite cleavage of opinion. Sixty-seven per cent of the headteachers and 59 per cent of the teachers

30

in the schools visited think that statutory religious education should be retained, and the proportion of those holding this opinion is greater in the voluntary schools than in the county schools. Twenty-five per cent of the atheists in the schools, 22 per cent of the agnostics, 30 per cent of the humanists, 54 per cent of the nominal Christians, and 71 per cent of the committed Christians believe that the law, as it stands at present, should continue to be enforced.

One reason commonly given for the retention of statutory religious education is the impoverishment children would experience if the subject disappeared from the curriculum. This is said by many teachers to be particularly the case today, when so few children have any church connexions. The following comment represents a number of similar statements: 'If children did not experience some sense of worship, wonder, and knowledge of the Christian faith in school, their lives would be greatly impoverished. We should not be helping them to realize their full potential.' Some teachers see the home background of many children as being in need of a counteracting influence in school, and they believe that Christian teaching and morning assemblies are valuable in creating this influence. A headteacher of a school in a deprived area makes this point, and adds, 'For many of our children the school assembly may be a place of peace and quiet, their sole experience of such an atmosphere.'

A few non-Christian teachers wish to see the removal of religious education from the school curriculum because they believe the tenets of religion to be false, and they do not want falsehood to be communicated to children; but most of those who oppose statutory religious education do so for reasons connected with those who teach it and the way in which they teach it. The following comments represent this expression of opinion: 'Religious education and compulsory assembly should be abolished. There is too much teaching of debased Christianity by uninterested people'; 'So many teachers feel uneasy or downright dishonest in teaching something about which they are themselves uncertain, that I am opposed to any form of compulsory religious education or assembly'; 'As a practising Christian I should like to see compulsory religious education abolished. The desire to make it acceptable to all leads to much watering down, and it is difficult to defend compulsion when staff opt out.'

The headmistress of a Roman Catholic infant school expressed a different point of view. She writes, 'The present controversy over the provision of religious education in school is being fought at adult level, and sometimes very subjectively. The children's needs are not always seen from their point of view. The abolitionists are perhaps letting certain prejudices blind them to the fact that most young children, given the chance, have a natural aptitude for belief and worship.'

31

Teachers vary considerably in their enjoyment of the religious education for which they are responsible. Four per cent of the headteachers and 11 per cent of the teachers in the schools visited said they found religious education to be less enjoyable than most of their other work in school, 56 per cent of headteachers and 78 per cent of teachers found it about as enjoyable, and 40 per cent of headteachers and 11 per cent of teachers more enjoyable. None of the atheists or agnostics enjoyed religious education more than their other work, but 4 per cent of the humanists, 6 per cent of the nominal Christians, and 21 per cent of the committed Christians said they did. Seventy-three per cent of the committed Christians regarded religious education as just about as pleasant to teach as the other subjects in the curriculum.

Table 3 (p. 76) shows that the number of teachers who withdraw from religious education is quite small. More teachers might take advantage of the option if they did not consider it disloyal to do so, although 98 per cent of the headteachers and 80 per cent of the teachers in the schools visited said they would not withdraw even if they were sure that their action would result in neither educational disturbance to the children nor inconvenience to other members of staff.

When asked to select from a list their greatest problem in religious education, 40 per cent of the 425 members of staff who responded to this question named the non-religious atmosphere of the children's home background as their first choice, 16 per cent named the difficulty of fitting religious education into the curriculum, and 12 per cent named their own religious beliefs. Seven per cent of the total staffs did not respond to the request, presumably because none of the items listed in the questionnaire corresponded to anything that presented a problem to them.

TEACHING ABOUT WORLD RELIGIONS

There were few definitive comments on the desirability of attempting to teach about world religions other than Christianity in the primary schools, and few positive aims in this field were stated. There seems to be a fairly general desire to extend religious teaching beyond Christianity to include some of the ideas in the other great religions of the world, but reservations abound in teachers' comments: there can be no success unless the teachers themselves are personally involved with the children in the search for meaning; an obvious bias towards Christianity will create the wrong impression; if the study is purely an academic exercise it will make little impact, etc. In one school, however, comparative religion is seen in an essentially practical way. The stress is on what each religion

32

has to offer to the others, and 'family worship' in the school community seeks to draw Muslims, Hindus, orthodox Jews, and Christians into a sense of kinship. In this school a group of 10-year-old children compiled a book of prayers drawn from the worship of three faiths; and two close friends, a Muslim and a Jew, produced jointly a beautifully coloured map of Palestine showing the positions of Christian, Muslim, and Jewish shrines.

Few teachers in the schools visited were attempting any kind of specific teaching of comparative religion, but experiences in one or two schools suggest that where there is a teacher ready to do some rethinking about the ways in which different people approach the mysteries of life, opportunities may occur in which a few of the more intelligent children become interested in, and derive some benefit from, an exploration in the simplest terms of other faiths.

MORAL EDUCATION

Broadly speaking, headteachers seem to envisage three main objectives in moral education for the primary school: **a** to help children to become well adjusted to life, socially and morally, and to establish good personal relationships; **b** to enable children to build healthy attitudes – kindness, love, unselfishness, courage, etc.; and **c** to establish a code of behaviour for life in the community, which will include the commonly accepted standards of society.

Twenty-eight per cent of the 422 members of staff of the schools visited who commented on the subject said that if compulsory religious education were abolished they would wish to teach moral education, while 70 per cent of them said they prefer to include moral education in their religious education scheme of work. This was expressed by one headteacher in these words: 'Moral education springs from religious teaching, which provides a standard by which conduct can be tested', and another, the head of a Roman Catholic infant school, is more explicit when she says, 'Instruction is based on the Fatherhood of God and the life of Christ.'

Some headteachers insist on the possibility of establishing a happy school community with high moral standards without bringing the Christian religion into it, while many teachers say that the low moral standards by which many children are surrounded out of school call for insistence on a firm moral code in school, and that in some cases this is as much as can be achieved. Most heads, whether Christian or not, agree that example is more important than instruction, and that sincerity on the part of the staff is all important. A few almost despair of doing anything in the way of moral training, partly because in so many cases home support is lacking, and partly because, as one of them said, 'social attitudes

33

are undergoing such change – I don't believe there are eternal truths in this field. We do not know exactly what is relevant to the primary-school child.'

ASSEMBLY IN THE PRIMARY SCHOOL

Morning assembly is the part of religious education in which both teachers and headteachers seem to be most confident that they are succeeding, perhaps because it is comparatively easy to introduce interesting variations within the given framework and thus to give an appearance of freshness and even of novelty to the exercise. This is often identified with 'success'. Many head-teachers, and nearly all the heads of infant schools who commented on the subject, see the daily assembly as the most vital part of a child's religious experience in school, and believe that it sets the tone for the rest of the day and influences the total atmosphere of the school community.

Assembly is highly regarded for its unifying influence, giving to the school a cohesion which it would otherwise lack, a family spirit and a feeling of 'togetherness'. Some believe that this is of the essence of worship 'even if the word God is not mentioned', but many say that if this community experience is shared with teachers to whom religious education has a vital meaning, children may be led into an awareness of God as a consequence of it.

One headteacher stresses the opinion that for young children assemblies should always be short, because of the intensity of the experience. She holds that it is 'this concentration of feeling which makes the service meaningful and uplifting – a valuable experience for children in an area where they will not meet this anywhere else'. The head of a church school speaks in glowing terms of the value of a school eucharist for junior children, in which they robe, carry candles, swing the censer, and take part in the offertory procession. He is firmly of the opinion that 10- and 11-year-olds can gain a good deal from a discussion of the symbolism involved in such a service, and that brightness, variety, and active participation may be the beginning of a lasting interest in the liturgy of the Church.

A number of headteachers, chiefly in junior schools, take a rather different line; they see assembly as an occasion for moral teaching. Here, one of them says, 'broad principles of behaviour and general moral teaching can constantly be put to the whole school.' The following are typical remarks: 'Morning assembly is the ideal opportunity for moral education as part of the wide scope of religious education'; 'Morning assembly is the tangible group situation which focuses on moral and religious ideals'; 'We use stories with a moral bias in assemblies'; 'Many children here are from deprived homes and tend to be very

34

aggressive – moral themes are used in assembly'; 'We use Bible stories sometimes, but any good story with a moral will do.'

Some heads think that daily assembly is too frequent for adequate preparation
to be made, and several refer to the difficulty of making assembly an act of real
worship where some of the staff show indifference or open opposition to it.
Others doubt whether children really 'worship' in most assemblies. The head of
a Roman Catholic school expressed the hope that pleasurable experiences might
spill over into worship, and ventured the opinion that young children probably
experience at least fleeting moments of worship from time to time.

THE BACKGROUND OF THE PUPILS

When the questionnaire invited teachers to say what they considered to be the
greatest problem facing them in attempting to give religious education in school,
40 per cent of them said, 'The non-religious background of the pupils.' Furthermore, in interviews with teachers and headteachers real concern about the
influence of the outside environment emerged so frequently that we must give
it considerable weight as a factor they consider significant in determining what
can be achieved in school. The three most commonly named external influences
are: **a** moral standards at home and in society which conflict with those the
school is seeking to establish; **b** a materialistic attitude to life; and **c** religious
unbelief or scepticism in parents and in people generally.

Almost without exception heads of schools in urban industrial areas had much
to say about the lack of moral stability in the home environment of their pupils.
In small schools and in rural areas the problem seems to be less acute, perhaps
because closer co-operation between school and home is possible and because
in a smaller school it is easier to create a family atmosphere. It is certainly true
that in small village schools home and school seem to pull together more amicably
and more effectively than in larger schools in industrial towns and cities. The
problem was said by some teachers to be acute in their own locality. In one
mining area it was reported that more than half of the children in a junior school
came from problem homes, and some of these children were disturbed sufficiently for it to affect their work in school.

Many headteachers believe that the existence and the intensity of these problems make the need to create an atmosphere of love and security in the school
community doubly important, and at the same time they greatly reduce the possibility of establishing relationships with the children based on mutual trust.

The second influence commented upon by a large number of headteachers
is the social outlook of children today, many of whom are brought up from their

earliest years against a background of getting and spending, of preoccupation with pleasure, and of the dominance of physical things. It is difficult to establish for such children an appreciation of the value of people for their own sake and not for what can be got from them. As one headmaster put it, 'Where parents are out to get what they can, where the attitude is something for nothing, give as good as you get, [then] encouragement of understanding, consideration for other people, and tolerance and forgiveness, can be formidable tasks.'

Another difficulty experienced by teachers today is that of helping children with a self-centred attitude to life to feel compassion for other people, to identify themselves imaginatively with those in trouble, and to come to the point of self-giving in love for others. Where children grow up never knowing hunger that is not quickly satisfied, and cushioned against the harsher experiences of life, it is difficult to get them beyond 'feeling sorry for' other people, or the idea of 'do-gooding,' to the point of experiencing genuine sympathetic understanding of the sufferings other people endure. Many schools try to stimulate an awareness of the needs of others by arranging for the children's contributions to be sent to organizations which help the unfortunate or the handicapped, and there is abundant evidence that this is done on an extensive scale by schools. This form of charity has its own dangers, however. A headteacher discussing it asked, 'Are we feeding the myth that if you put in your money your obligation to your brother is discharged?'

The third matter of concern to headteachers and teachers of religion is parental unbelief, which is frequently reflected in children. Primary-school pupils today are sometimes heard to say, 'My dad says God-stuff is a load of old rubbish', or something similar. An experienced headteacher of a junior school in a wealthy middle-class area said she had never before known so many un-believing children. Many children of 8, 9, or 10 years old are sceptical about the truth of the Bible. This critical attitude seems to be growing. One teacher's account of the biblical story of the creation was greeted by an 8-year-old who said, 'God didn't make the world like that: there was a big explosion', and the same teacher was informed when she told the story of the Flood that if Noah lived so long ago, the animals would not be sheep and cows and monkeys, but 'dinosaurs and things'. To children of today in a school of this kind, heart transplants are much more exciting achievements than the far-away stories of the miracles of Jesus. In another junior school 10- and 11-year-olds raised the problem of evil. One of them said, 'If God made everything he must have made the bad things too.'

36

2. The school visits

We spent two days in most of the fifty-six schools visited, saw a great deal of religious teaching in progress, and attended something like a hundred assemblies. In addition, schools had at our request generously preserved for our inspection some of the children's work done previously, and in a few cases had recorded on tape some of their assemblies and discussions. In this section of the report a few general observations will be made, and in the next section actual examples of teaching and assemblies will be cited and briefly commented upon.

CLASSROOM ACTIVITIES

Most professional teachers have thought for a long time that Bible stories are particularly vulnerable to misunderstanding by children, and Goldman's work in the 1960s confirmed, to the satisfaction of many educationists, the truth of this opinion. Goldman's forthright declaration that 'the Bible is not a children's book' had the effect at first of deterring some teachers from telling Bible stories to young children, but the effect seems partly to have worn off by now. In all but two of the schools visited we found stories from the Bible being told more or less freely at some time or another, and in one of these two infant schools where biblical material was deliberately avoided, a concession was made at Christmas. Some schools, for example two rural Welsh-speaking schools and the only two preparatory schools we saw, emphatically base their religious education on the Bible.

It has to be remembered that Goldman reached his conclusions as a result of his investigations with randomly selected pupils, and not with pupils from schools where the religious education was known to be above average. In the schools we visited, chosen by nominators because they considered that the religious education in these schools was above average, we often saw biblical material being used.

The myths of Genesis 1–11 are taught in many primary schools, and inevitably received at infant stage as if they are literally true. This is especially the case with the story of Noah's ark, which seems to be considered by many teachers to be too good a story to omit. It is sometimes even bolstered up by an appeal to 'archaeology', and it is a favourite subject for art and craft expression work. The very skill with which it is taught and impressed on the minds of young children in many infant and junior schools may make the shock all the greater when a child awakens to the fact that it is not to be regarded as literally true.

In addition to stories from the Bible, stories of the lives of Christian saints and

37

heroes figure largely in primary-school religious education, the assumption being that they illustrate the work of the Holy Spirit in the lives of men and women from New Testament times to the present day. These stories are enjoyed especially by juniors, and they are readily accessible in the standard collections of children's stories.

Four teaching operations were observed in religious education, any of which may be used in either a timetabled or an 'integrated day' context:

1   a story or other activity restricted to one short period;
2   a cross-subject activity restricted to one short period;
3   an unrestricted series of periods in which a topic that is within the child's experience is explored;
4   an unrestricted series of periods in which related subjects are explored, usually by different teachers.

Most examples in the first category followed suggestions from either an agreed or a diocesan syllabus, but a few schools had prepared schemes of work for their own use. The headmistress of a northern county school devises a different syllabus each year and distributes copies to her teachers. These syllabuses are based on the local education authority's agreed syllabus, and the annual variations are aimed at preventing the staleness that sometimes sets in when teachers have to handle the same material in the same way year after year.

The first kind of lesson is usually planned as an isolated unit; but it might be unplanned and prompted by an event inside or outside the school, or by the chance remark of a teacher or a child. The teacher judges when it is right to abandon or postpone a planned lesson for a spontaneous one.

In the second method a teacher with a wide range of knowledge breaks down the usual barriers between subjects and moves easily from one to the other, assuming that everything is interrelated.

The third method is the one we saw in use most often. It is the thematic method recommended in the new type of agreed syllabus and in several handbooks. Although it is widely used, it is by no means universal. Many schools tried it when it was first suggested in Goldman's writings, but some of them have been disappointed with it and have abandoned it. One headmaster was sure that they had a set of theme-teaching booklets in the school somewhere – but they were so deeply buried in the store-room that they could not be found in a prolonged search! This would probably be the case in many other schools. The main cause of complaint is that the booklets do not contain sufficient religion to justify their use in religious education. A teacher of 7-year-olds said, 'Last year we went all round this town looking at people who cared for us: postmen,

38

firemen, bakers. The children loved it, but the small religious element worried me. With some thematic booklets it's just the same. The whole term's work can lead up to an artificially dragged-in religious education slot just before the end.' A teacher of 10-year-olds in another school said, 'The trouble with this thematic series is that if a child sneezes and is off school for one day, he might miss the term's religious education!'

Our observations and discussions with groups of teachers compel us to say that many of those who have abandoned theme teaching, and not a few of those who continue to use it, have probably never thought out the implications of the method and therefore have an inadequate understanding of it. This may be due to ineffective communication on the part of its exponents or to a weakness in some of the material intended for use in the class room, but the most likely cause of the trouble is the teachers' insufficient grasp of the theology involved in the method.

Our observations on theme teaching are to be found elsewhere in this report (pp. 59ff.).

The fourth method is sometimes called team teaching. It is a method more suited to the secondary school where subject specialists abound, but it is being successfully applied in some of the primary schools we visited and it is therefore worth a brief mention here. In this method a group of teachers deal with the same subject from different points of view: literary, artistic, scientific, historical, geographical, and religious.

No school in our experience has developed a scheme of work in moral education either inside or outside the framework of religious education. It seems generally to be assumed that moral education can be given informally and incidentally, and that it is the responsibility of all the members of staff whenever the opportunity for it arises. Nor has any school we visited in which there are non-Christian immigrant children made any attempt to introduce religious education of the kind that would be acceptable to the parents of these pupils. There are signs, however, that this issue is likely to assume greater importance in the near future if immigrant groups decide to make use of their legal right of withdrawal.

ASSEMBLIES

The 1944 Education Act says that every 'school day . . . shall begin with . . . a single act of worship' attended by all the pupils in the school, but we rarely found an infant school where assembly was held at 9 a.m., and we visited several schools in which separate assemblies were held for infants and juniors. Some headteachers would like to reduce the frequency of assemblies to two or three

39

a week, and in one school the headmistress declares an 'assembly fast' for several days when the situation seems to require it. Whenever these matters were discussed, the breaches of the law were defended on what seemed to us to be sound educational or religious grounds.

Many county primary schools seem to have broken away almost completely from the traditional type of hymn-singing, and hymns with contemporary words and music are now widely used. In a few schools hymns of high quality composed by members of staff are effectively sung. On the whole, the hymns and prayers we heard in the county schools were comparatively free from archaisms, pictorial crudities, and high-density metaphor. Where voluntary schools are closely bound by the liturgy of the Church, the situation is obviously different, but here also there are refreshing breaks with tradition in some church schools.

The assemblies in the schools we visited were of three kinds:

1 daily routine assemblies;
2 occasional special assemblies;
3 festival celebrations.

The first kind were usually conducted by the headteacher or by another member of staff, but the second kind were frequently arranged and conducted by pupils. Clergy and ministers in aided schools, and sometimes by invitation in controlled and county schools, occasionally conducted the third kind of assembly.

Aided schools sometimes meet in church for their morning worship, as the 1946 Education Act gives them the right to do, although it is made clear that normally the school is the proper meeting place for this purpose.

3. Examples of observed religious education

The following briefly-described examples are quoted as representative of the kind of religious education we saw in the schools we visited. Not all of them are to be wholeheartedly commended. The form taken by these activities was usually determined by local circumstances, and they therefore cannot be re-enacted in the same form in schools where the circumstances are different. It should also be remembered that the written accounts cannot reproduce the verve, the gestures, the tone of voice or the personality of the teacher and that they are thereby seriously impoverished and cannot give an adequate impression of the occasions they describe.

Comments on some of these examples will be found on pp. 53ff.

1. An end-of-afternoon story
There were thirty-seven children, aged 5 to 7, sitting round the teacher in this large family-grouped county infant school. She asked, 'Who helps me?', and the children answered in chorus, 'We do.' 'Who helps the headmistress?', 'The teachers.' The story was about some baby birds in 'a warm strong nest' that was blown by a gale into a stream. The birds floated in the nest and were rescued and cared for by two boys. During and after the story there was uninhibited questioning by the children, and an immigrant child of above-average intelligence showed concern for the mother bird's 'feelings'. The children said together, 'Thank you for those who help us,' and in a short silence that followed the teacher suggested that they should thank God for any people they knew who help others.

2. The burning bush incident
A class of twenty-seven 8-year-old boys of above-average intelligence in a preparatory school went through the incident of the burning bush with their teacher, the religious education specialist for half the school, answering her questions on the biblical text from which they had read the story. Later in the day they answered in writing other questions on the incident to test their general understanding of it.

3. The story of the lost sheep
This story from Luke 15 was told in Welsh to the reception class of a rural primary school. It was then dramatized, drawn in crayon, and the drawings were labelled by the teacher and pasted into a book entitled 'Stori o'r Beibl' ('A Story from the Bible').

4. Care for a snail
A 7-year-old boy on the path outside the classroom was about to tread on a snail to kill it. The teacher restrained the boy by encouraging him to look at the snail in a new way. She drew his attention to its silver trail, the marking on its shell, and the curious way in which it 'walks' without legs. Within two days the children had established a small colony of snails and were caring for them. They could be heard saying, 'Be careful, don't tread on him.'

5. The rosy apples
The teacher showed her class of 8- and 9-year-old children a bowl of lovely rosy apples and they enjoyed the beauty of them together. She then cut one apple in half and the children examined the pips in the seed-box and discussed the

41

growth of an apple tree from a pip. The teacher then told the story of an old woman who had a small apple tree which bore twenty apples one year. She gathered the apples and stored them for her own use. One day a coach-load of twenty handicapped children stopped at the door and asked for a drink of water. The old woman was sorry for them and gave each of the children one of her precious apples. The teacher told the class, 'The children were happy, the nurse in charge of them was happy – and even the old woman was happy! Perhaps Jesus would have been happy if he had been there.'

Next, the verse which begins 'The ripe fruit in the garden . . .' was sung from the hymn 'All things bright and beautiful', and the rosy apples were cut in pieces by the teacher and distributed by two children to the rest of the class – and to the observer! When all had received a piece of apple, we ate together and finally said a short prayer together.

6. Power
Encouraged by the teacher, this class of 9-year-olds in a large Roman Catholic school in an industrial area suggested examples of mechanical power: locomotive, steam-hammer, dynamo, jet-plane, etc. Further discussion enabled them to suggest examples of a different kind: the power of personality, persuasion, public opinion, etc. Finally, the power of God was discussed, and the teacher illustrated it by referring to the process of evolution (although the word itself was not mentioned). Using the thought of Teilhard de Chardin (but not naming him, of course) the teacher put forward the suggestion that the energy in all the stages of evolution from inanimate matter to animate beings is the power of God at work in the world of nature.

7. Beauty
In this example thematic teaching was used on a wide scale, in a project on the subject of beauty. All the children in this Welsh infant school took part in this during the summer term – considered by the staff to be a suitable time of year for such a subject. It is too long to report in full, but the following brief outline represents the stages in the work undertaken by a class of 7- and 8-year-olds. The same subject was dealt with by the lower classes at the appropriate level of their understanding and experience.

Prayers of the 'Thank you, God . . .' type were said by the teacher and children at every stage of the project.

Nature. Children's experience of beautiful things in nature (grass, flowers, trees, etc.) – a class excursion – collection of flowers and foliage to decorate the classroom – hymn ('In the lanes and in the parks') – model of the local park made

42

by the class – plants and flowers Jesus saw in Palestine – colour in the Holy Land contrasted with colour in our own country – the colour of hair, eyes, faces of class companions.

Fashion. The clothes we wear compared with Eastern dress and clothing in Jesus' time – story (Joseph and his coat of many colours) – favourite colours – the most popular and the least popular colours in the opinion of the class – colours in the sky.

Space. Colours of the sun, moon, stars – hymn ('Twinkle, twinkle, little star') – space travel – colours of the burning gas as a rocket takes off – metallic colours of the space-craft – model of a space station made by boys – background frieze of stars and planets made by girls.

Sea. Summer holidays coming soon – colours of the sea, fish, shells, etc. – frieze of sea treasures made by the class – hymn ('When lamps are lighted in the town') – story (the fishermen of Galilee) – a thank-you prayer.

Movement. The restless sea – movement of swaying seaweed – children's actions to represent these movements – other beautiful movement (bird flight, ballet dancers, footballers, etc.).

Sounds. Different pitch of voices of class companions – beautiful and ugly sounds illustrated by the children – favourite sounds (cat purring, kettle boiling, bees buzzing, rain falling, etc.) – a hymn may be a beautiful sound ('All things bright and beautiful').

Kindness. The beauty of 'being nice to someone' – recollection of deeds of kindness shown or received during the past week – story (the good Samaritan).

Forgiveness. This was found to be too difficult for this age group, and it could only be illustrated by a story (the prodigal son).

Friendship. Examples of friendship – stories of friendship, biblical and non-biblical.

Each child produced a booklet, 'My Book of Beauty', in which ideas were recorded; pictures, friezes, and models were made; and a Hymn of Beauty was composed and sung at assembly.

8. Roads

This is the junior-school part of an experiment organized by a teachers' centre to link the religious education in neighbouring primary and secondary schools.

The story of roads. Ancient bridges – Roman roads – Hadrian's Wall – modern roads.

Help on the road. Police – AA and RAC – traffic wardens – inns and hotels.

Stories of travel in Bible times. Joseph's Journey to Egypt – the flight into Egypt with baby Jesus – roads to Jericho, Emmaus, and Damascus – inns.

9. Creation

The humanist teacher of these 9- and 10-year-old children in a voluntary school in a rural area is able to use her considerable gifts in art and craft to produce excellent work folders. This was a one-term exercise on the subject of Creation.

Creation and movement. Birds, fish, stars – story (Sketco the raven) – the mechanics of writing.

Musical instruments. These were used to simulate stars bursting in the sky, warriors celebrating the birth of a baby, release of the sun and moon in the sky.

Myths of creation. Maori, Babylonian, West African, Icelandic, and Hebrew stories of creation.

Science. Archaeological and geological discoveries.

10. Psalm 150

This class of 8-year-old juniors in a voluntary school considered Psalm 150 during the autumn term as a preparation for Christmas. A wide range of expression was used: writing, drawing, mime, and dance.

Creation. Four boys produced a large frieze depicting the Hebrew view of creation in the psalm (verses 1 and 2).

Music. The instruments mentioned in the psalm were drawn, constructed, and played to accompany mime and dance, with the rest of the school as audience (verses 3–5).

Doxology. The Gloria in the psalm was portrayed in a colourful frieze showing 'every thing that hath breath' offering praise to God (verse 6).

11. Blindness

The teacher of this class of 10- and 11-year-old children in a rural voluntary school is a humanist. She has musical interest and ability, which she used effectively in this work of preparation for the following week's assembly.

Writing. About ten children composed poems and prose passages on topics stimulated by the story of Helen Keller: 'Hands and voices'; 'Going blind'; 'A blind person going out for the first time'; 'Guide dogs'.

Music. Another group of children composed verses to a catchy tune composed jointly by the teacher and some members of the class. The teacher also composed the music of an effective refrain: 'Eyes, eyes . . .'.

12. An approach to the Bible

The following outline represents an extended exercise which took place in a large county junior school with a good cross-section of children from working-class and middle-class homes.

44

Biblical myths. A class of 10- and 11-year-old children studied the stories in Genesis 1–11. They discovered that they contain early Hebrew answers to man's questions about the origin of pain, evil, and hatred in the world.

Non-biblical myths. The myths of other peoples were studied, and they were found to deal with the same questions as the Hebrew myths, but the answers were different from the Hebrew answers.

The Old Testament. The lives of some of the Old Testament heroes (Moses, Joshua, David, and others) were studied and used to illustrate God's desire to deliver his people from evil and to help them to live peaceably and happily.

The New Testament. Jesus of Nazareth was the supreme illustration of God's desire to save his people. An anthology of written work, mainly high quality poetry, was produced, and under the title, 'O come, let us adore him', was professionally printed and bound in paperback.

13. Living together

In this large county junior school three second-year groups engaged in a team-teaching experiment involving geography, history, mathematics, science, creative activities, music, dance-drama, and religious education. The Old Testament story of Joseph was used to contrast unhappy and happy family life, and it was linked with the teaching of Jesus in the New Testament.

Childrens' experience. Living together at home and in school with relatives and friends – selfish and unselfish attitudes.

Joseph. The story in detail, leading from the account of the unhappy family in Canaan to the account of the happily reunited family in Egypt.

The teaching of Jesus. Forgiveness, loyalty, trust, love, etc.

Children's experience. Living together at home and in school reconsidered in the light of the teaching of Jesus – living in the community and in the world.

Group work was done on the following themes: group 1, *The lands of Palestine and Egypt* – life in the countryside, farming, nomads, fishermen, etc., water, irrigation (experiments were conducted by the class on evaporation, seed germination, plant life, colour); group 2, *The people* – merchants, slaves, workmen, craftsmen, magicians, etc., clothes, homes, work; group 3, *Customs* – gods, pyramids, mourning, embalming, writing, the calendar, measurements, temples, etc.

14. Sharing bread

This assembly took place in the spacious hall of a voluntary school two weeks before the harvest festival. The junior assembly had been held earlier in the morning, and this assembly was for about one hundred infants, including a reception class.

The children walked into the hall quietly with no entrance music. The headmaster said a very short opening prayer, and then reminded the children of the subject of the two previous assemblies: things which grow, leading to 'corn makes bread'. 'Here's some corn' (holding it up in his hand) 'but we haven't any bread . . . Or, have we? . . .' (the children couldn't see any) 'Look round the hall and see if you can find any.' Hesitantly at first, the children moved away, then more boldly they went from place to place with bursts of running, changes of direction, pauses; with eager, puzzled looks on their faces, but with very few words. The headmaster had discreetly placed small slices of bread on ledges and on chairs, and when all of it had been found the children drifted back to their original places. 'What's bread for?' asked the head. 'Eating!' 'Well, eat it then . . . Oh! wait. Some children haven't got any . . .' (deliberately only enough slices for about half the children had been put out) 'What can we do about that?' 'Share it', volunteered one or two timid voices. Those who had found a piece of bread broke it in half, and sometimes in half again, and shared it until all had a piece. 'Shall we say a prayer before we eat it?', and a short prayer followed. 'Let's sing a hymn as we eat.' The children sang and nibbled, and smiled at one another and at the headteacher. The children then moved quietly to their classes.

15. The rainbow

This assembly was taken entirely by children of the infant department in this county school, but teachers had obviously given considerable help in the preparation.

There was a backcloth representing Noah's ark, with the animals and an enormous rainbow. At one side there was a large blank space. During the playing of a record ('I can sing a rainbow') four children pinned large, brightly coloured flowers on the blank section of the backcloth. The children were dressed in rainbow-coloured crepe paper, each one a different colour. A simplified version of the Noah story was read, emphasizing the part about the rainbow. The song, 'Who built the ark? Noah! Noah!' was sung, and six short prayers were said, expressing thanks for different colours. The prayers were down to earth: the boy in blue, for example, was grateful for the colour blue, because it was the colour of his father's car and of his favourite football club.

16. Roses

There were far too many children for the hall in this large county school – it took nearly ten minutes to pack them all in – and there were also thirty to forty

46

mothers at the assembly with their younger children. The presence of mothers is a weekly feature. In spite of the large number of children the arrangements went very smoothly.

There was a large bowl of roses on the table, and the headmaster had a large rose in his buttonhole. He told the story of the production during the war of the rose 'Peace', and how it came to have that name. There was a rousing rendering of the hymn, 'For all the saints', and a formal prayer. An excellent school orchestra (violins, cellos, clarinets, trombone – and even a double bass!) played 'Mary and Judas'.

17. Keeping the right time

Clocks and watches of many different sizes, colours, and faces had been modelled and were on display in this infant school assembly. Each had a caption: 'I am right', 'I am slow', etc. Several children read what they had previously written about the kind of people they would like to be (having different characteristics – like the clocks and watches) when they grew up. A hymn was accompanied on chime-bars, and a solo piece was played.

18. Caring

This was one of a series of assemblies in a large county junior school, dealing with different aspects of caring. A group of children recited in chorus, 'The wolf cub and the grizzly bear', a sad story of a little cub who thought he knew better than his elders, was disobedient, and came to a bad end. This was offset by a story told by the headteacher about his rabbit, Snowy, who escaped from his hutch and had a feast in a neighbour's garden. The neighbour was angry and threatened to kill Snowy if he came into his garden again. So Snowy's hutch had to be very securely locked, for his own sake. Parents sometimes have to say 'no' to things we want, for our own sake, because they love us.

19. Racial harmony

This was a dramatic presentation given at Christmas in a county primary school with a large number of immigrant children. Parents were present.

The traditional nativity play was abandoned, and this version of it was substituted. A West Indian couple who had been evicted from their home were expecting a baby. They were offered a room by a Greek Cypriot family until they could find a house in which to live. The final tableau had as its centre a large cross held up by two children, one coloured and the other white. On one side of the cross were Mary, Joseph, and the baby Jesus: on the other side the West Indian couple and their baby. Surrounding them were other children, arranged alternately coloured and white.

4. Comments on the school visits ⟨Cm + Cmj⟩

THE TEACHERS

The first comment must be in admiration of the sincerity, devotion, and professional skill which the great majority of the teachers in the schools we visited bring to their work in religious education. Some of the school buildings in which they work are old and inadequate, and they are situated in deprived areas where there is little help from the environment and almost none from parents. Yet in spite of these adverse conditions very many teachers make a valiant attempt to create in their schools an atmosphere in which children can experience security and affection, and in which they can explore religious beliefs and practices in an enjoyable and effective way.

Having said that, in all sincerity, something must be added about the biblical and theological point of view of these teachers, for we believe it has a profound effect on the quality of the religious education in the schools.

Where teachers declared themselves to be Christian, a majority of them appeared to be conservative in theological outlook and in their approach to the Bible. Only a mere handful of those who, in our hearing, told stories about Jesus, for example, gave any indication of having thought or read much about the kind of literature the gospels are, about the nature of the material with which the gospel writers were dealing, or about the religious significance of Bible stories for children in the primary school today. Similarly, stories from the Old Testament were often heard in both the infant and the junior schools, told by teachers who lacked the necessary theological insight or the critical knowledge to present them as anything more than dramatic incidents, historical episodes, or moral tales.

There are, of course, primary-school teachers who approach the Bible in a way which is likely to promote deeper understanding, but in our experience they are rare. In general there is little evidence among teachers in primary schools of positive theological thinking and little awareness of the trends in recent biblical scholarship. This is not surprising, nor are teachers themselves wholly to blame: in most cases they have not been trained in these subjects (see Table 2, p. 76) and they therefore cannot be expected to be proficient in them. Nevertheless, a teacher who is retarded in his own religious thinking and who is largely ignorant of the kind of material he is handling can scarcely hope to bring children to an appreciation of its religious significance. The teacher's ignorance in this field may hinder him from being able to help children in their search for meaning. Not infrequently we have seen teachers in a situation where, like Marcion, they had two Gods: the God of the Old Testament and the God of the New

48

Testament. This is embarrassing for the teacher and it may be potentially harmful in its effect on the child's later thinking about God.

THE INFLUENCE OF THE HEADTEACHER

Our observations clearly show that the headteacher can play a vital part in the religious education in a primary school, and some of the ways in which we saw this influence being exerted are set out below.

There are some schools where a homely atmosphere is experienced from the first moments of a visit; where warmth and friendliness from head, staff, and children reach out immediately to embrace a stranger. Without exception, it is found that the headteachers of such schools are decisively, and sometimes purposefully, creating relationships that are themselves the explanation of the atmosphere. These are men and women of vision; sometimes, but by no means always, of Christian conviction; with a positive, well-thought-out philosophy of education, and a genuine concern for people.

Some of these heads have compelling personal qualities and the gift of awakening a response in others, so that working with them enlarges horizons, broadens knowledge, and sharpens perception. Such men and women can weld together into a working team members of staff with dissimilar temperament, experience and ability; and within such a team individuals can be helped to grow in self-knowledge, can become aware of their strengths and weaknesses, and can learn to share resources with other members of the team. They can be brought to see that there is no arbitrary right or wrong way of doing most things, but that children learn from varied approaches. The need is for headteachers to ensure that there is balance and co-ordination in the work of the school, and to this end they should have a clear picture of the overall impact that they hope religious education will have on the children.

The key to success in this aspect of education is the headteacher's knowledge of his staff and the children they teach. Several heads, with this in mind, make a point of going round the school every day to see what is happening, and of always being available to their staff and open to receive suggestions from them.

From our discussions with headteachers two of their concerns emerge. The first is the need to ensure that there is among the staff of a school a blending of different kinds of experience; so that teachers who are set in their ways may learn how to adopt new approaches to religious education, and inexperienced young teachers may learn from their more experienced colleagues how to acquire a deeper understanding of children and their needs. The headteacher can do a great deal towards establishing this kind of harmonious co-operation

49

by making known his appreciation of what individual teachers contribute to the common good, and of the value of different viewpoints in helping to arrive at a balanced planning of the curriculum.

The second concern is expressed by headteachers who are anxious to move away from the older, more traditional ways of teaching religious education towards the integration of religious activities with other kinds of activities within the school situation. A few headteachers who have themselves recognized the value of this approach are actively challenging teachers of different experience, temperament, and conviction to do some radical re-thinking along these lines.

Most headteachers said that they were aiming at some measure of integration of work in their schools. Often this seemed to mean no more than a disregard of the classical subject boundaries and an absence of rigid timetabling, or an attempt to relate the various aspects of the curriculum to one another. That real integration means much more than this is clear from a long statement, well worth quoting from, by a group of Shropshire teachers:

> Work grows from a challenging stimulus, the children using many avenues of discovery and different media for recording their findings. Many subjects are used in a meaningful and purposive way to seek after knowledge. The religious element takes its place and makes a valid contribution to the whole. The starting-point may be religious experience, or the sharing of the completed work may be religious experience. It is helpful to think of children's spiritual growth rather than of their religious education.

Some heads are uncertain about the extent to which integration can be adopted. Many would limit it to the moderate degree mentioned above, and perhaps only a few are ready to go as far as the Shropshire teachers suggest. One headteacher expresses not only caution but also good sense when he says, 'Any change must only be carried through with understanding both of the needs of the children and the capabilities of the staff. Understanding of what we are doing is crucial.'

The practical advice which some heads give to their teachers who find an integrated approach difficult reflects some of their own concerns. Foremost is the problem of working out the best way of keeping records, so that teachers can guard against the overlapping of work, and can be sure that each child is covering a sufficiently wide range of study. Closely allied to this is the need to stimulate in teachers a sense of purpose, insight, and perceptiveness. When does one guide a child, and when leave him to his own experimentation? What constitutes guidance in this sense? One headteacher's answer to the latter question is that it is 'caring for the good of the children', and he adds, 'the teacher must learn

50

to keep a balance between allowing freedom for initiative and ensuring that basic skills are being learnt.' Several heads define guidance as giving 'freedom with discipline', or as 'freedom within a framework of security, so that children may come to self-discipline.'

Another fear of a different kind was sometimes expressed: namely, that when integration is adopted religion may be squeezed out or at least largely neglected, either because of the unbelief of the teacher or because religion is not recognized as an integral part of the whole of experience. With this in mind some heads offer specific suggestions to help their teachers towards a greater awareness of what can be done.

A few headteachers, concerned at the little that can be done in the face of the contemporary pressures discussed elsewhere (pp. 35–6), see the only way of enabling children to grow towards wholeness to be an even wider application of the principle of integration than was suggested by the Shropshire teachers mentioned above. This is nothing less than an integration of the school into its environment. In some small rural schools this can happen naturally and fairly easily: in urban and industrial areas it must be helped to happen by exercising a positive effort to establish trust and co-operation between school and home, and by stimulating a sense of urgency to help children to recognize standards of right and wrong, and to establish good relationships in the community.

To heads such as these it is useless to talk of integration within the school only. They envisage an outward-looking integration, with school learning and experience linked as closely as possible with the neighbourhood. In three schools we visited, two in London and one in the North, each presenting special problems, the headteachers are co-operating with clergy, welfare workers, and social workers on neighbourhood care committees. One head took the initiative in urging the town clerk to bring together representatives of all the bodies concerned: welfare visitors, doctors, police, magistrates, youth workers, etc. This group tried to hammer out a workable liaison between the various departments so that the school could be made fully aware of the social background of its children, become better able to understand their particular needs, and know how to meet them. The heads and some of the teachers in these schools visit homes where there is adversity, and parents visit the school for advice on a wide range of problems. This kind of situation makes integration looked at simply as a non-fragmenting of experience in school seem a pale shadow of what it might be. In the communities described above there is positive, purposeful cohesion of all the influences that may contribute to a child's healthy growth towards wholeness.

Several heads of the schools we visited have tried to work out ways of helping parents to understand the aims and the methods of modern primary-school education. In one school mothers of young children are encouraged to visit the school on one afternoon a week to 'have a go' alongside their children as they paint, model, or play. Some heads have organized meetings of parents to explain to them the New Mathematics, and others invite parents to bring their younger children to share in the morning assembly for worship. Most headteachers feel that their availability to parents is one of their most important responsibilities in spite of the fact that it is time-consuming and tiring work.

The heads of two of the schools we visited in which integration of this more extensive kind is to be seen at its most successful both stressed that it can be kept up for only part of the time, perhaps only for one term in the school year. They regard it as a climax to be worked towards, and its achievement a cause for congratulation.

Integration depends on people, and people in a school are constantly on the move: there are frequent changes of staff, older children go and new children come. It takes time for the head to get to know new teachers, children, and parents, and for teachers to get to know each other. It is necessary for the head to discover each teacher's talents and inclinations, and the teachers themselves must find the colleagues with whom they can work most happily in joint enterprises. Above all, a framework of trust and confidence has to be created within which all the members of the community can feel secure and able to venture freely – and this is not done in a day. Many modern educationists would say that all this, and the community living for which it is the preparation, is an essential part of religious education in the primary school of today, and to achieve it as fully as possible is one of the goals for which teachers and headteachers should aim.

Some heads who favour a thematic approach to religious education try to help their teachers to use the method effectively. There is some confusion about what constitutes a theme, and this is dealt with elsewhere (pp. 59ff.), but most headteachers accept the idea that religion is part of the wholeness of being and that it must not be separated from the rest of human experience. One headmaster suggests a possible idea for a theme to his staff, and by discussing the different ways in which it could develop helps his teachers to discover the religious elements in the theme, to decide if these should be made explicit, and to consider how the work should grow. Each teacher's relationship with the class has unique possibilities, so there can be no common planning, but by constant suggestion and discussion of this kind teachers are helped to a more sensitive understanding of theme teaching and of the learning capabilities of the children with whom they use it.

In the light of these and other factors in the present situation a few critical comments must now be made on the religious education in the schools we visited. If some of the comments seem negative, it should be noted that Chapter VI contains our positive suggestions for a valid approach to the subject.

AMBIVALENCE

The kind of ambivalence found in the sections of the Plowden and the Gittins Reports dealing with religious education, and in much of the writing about religious education that has appeared in recent years (pp. 17ff. above), is reflected, not surprisingly, in the attitudes to religious education of many of the teachers and headteachers in the primary schools we visited. In practice, this shows itself as a general uncertainty about the aims of religious education, and a corresponding uncertainty in classroom procedure on the part of some teachers.

As mentioned earlier, Goldman's somewhat technical account of his research appeared in book form in 1964 under the title *Religious Thinking from Childhood to Adolescence* (Routledge & Kegan Paul). Our discussions with primary-school teachers showed that not many of them had studied the book closely, but some of them had read popular summaries of its findings. Most of those who disagree with Goldman's radical theology were very little or not at all influenced by his work, but others readily accepted his suggestion when they first met it that the use of all but the very simplest Bible stories in the primary school is at best questionable and at worst positively harmful. Accordingly, the Bible was hastily jettisoned in many schools and hopes rose high that a stumbling-block to sound religious education had thus been removed. That was nearly ten years ago, and many of those who then so confidently adopted Goldman's thesis are now not so sure of its wisdom. They fear that by eliminating Bible teaching they may have eliminated religious teaching. Some of these disappointed teachers are therefore bringing back into their religious education the 'religious' elements which they believe it ought to contain: religious vocabulary, Bible teaching, and Christian worship. This tendency is clearly seen in several of the examples of religious education described above.

In example 7 (pp. 42-3), typical of several similar exercises observed during the school visits, the teaching was on the whole firmly and properly based on experience. The children were emotionally involved in satisfying ways and this kind of experimental learning was entirely appropriate for the stage of development most of them had reached. The religious content of the teaching was implicit in the theme; in such subjects, here only baldly stated, as Creation, Providence, the interdependence of mankind, the brotherhood of man, and love of God and neighbour. Teachers who were aware of this implicit religious content did not need to make it explicit by using technical religious terms, which would, in any case, have been incomprehensible to most of the children. Other teachers, however, felt constrained to invite the children to say thank-you prayers to God at the end of each section of the project. The danger in this is that the impression is given to the children that saying prayers is 'religious', that they must expect religion to be incomprehensible, and that the interesting part of the work has nothing to do with religion. Teachers who do not recognize the religious content in the theme itself will probably consider that it would not qualify as religious education if prayers were not said at every stage of the exercise.

Further comment on theme teaching is to be found on p. 59ff., and on children and prayer on pp. 67–8.

A similar situation was evident in some of the assemblies we saw. Example 16 (pp. 46–7) is a case in point, and it will serve to introduce the subject of hymn-singing in assembly. A suitable topic was chosen and it was dealt with in a lively and helpful way. Then a hymn was sung, a hymn of a theologically sophisticated kind ('For all the saints') that might be admirable for adults but which is quite incomprehensible to children in a primary school. Perhaps the presence of parents at this assembly was thought to justify the selection of this hymn on this occasion, but a hymn or a song closer to the children's level of understanding – the assembly had a flower theme – would have been more appropriate.

This gives us the opportunity to say, however, that we do not consider that intellectually inappropriate material is also necessarily emotionally valueless. The opposite is often the case: the impact of music, colour, and movement in a learning situation may be more significant for a young child than its intellectual content. It seems to be the case in hymn-singing that most children enjoy a good tune and that many of them take very little notice of the words they sing. This is probably equally true of the secular songs which they sing. This does not, however, completely release teachers and headteachers from their responsibility of selecting hymns and songs for children to sing in which the tune is pleasant and the words contain as few archaisms, obscure metaphors, and difficult technical words as possible.

Clearly, the subject of worship, including prayer, in the primary school is in urgent need of investigation, for we know almost nothing for certain about its effect on young children. Until such investigation has been completed, we dare not be dogmatic in our comments. What we have written on the subject in this and other chapters of this report must be read for what it is – namely, our subjective impression – and it must obviously stand open to correction in the light of future research (see our recommendation 1b, p. 69).

THE USE OF THE BIBLE

A brief examination of example 2 (p. 41) will illustrate what may be a general principle under this heading.

This preparatory school frankly bases its religious education on Bible teaching, and the boys showed themselves to be unusually familiar with at least the Old Testament. They quickly found Exodus 3 in their well-thumbed Bibles, and most of them were able to discuss intelligently the details in the story of the burning bush.

The written test revealed a number of misconceptions about the meaning of deity, awe, and holiness, but the interesting thing was that all but one of the twenty-seven boys spent considerable time and effort in explaining the mystery of the bush in non-literal terms: "The bush did not burn because it was a vision'; 'It looked as if it was burning'; 'The bush that Moses saw was in his head'; 'God seemed to speak from the bush, but it could have been in his head'; and so on. In contrast, ten of the twenty-seven boys failed to mention the nature of the call that came to Moses. These ten boys concentrated on the non-rational part of the story at the expense of the factual and the religiously significant part of it. They grappled with the intellectually puzzling details, but did not use a simple effort of memory to recall the main purpose for which the story was told. Could this not be a more frequent result of giving intelligent children 'too much too soon' (to use Goldman's phrase) than we sometimes allow? It is not only that, like the children with whom Goldman conducted his experiments, they cannot fully understand the meaning of abstract ideas, but that, in spite of their intelligence in other directions, they also lack the ability to distinguish the degrees of significance in an incident. With these ten boys in this class the unusual element in the story took on an undue importance in their thinking and remained in their memories more clearly than the elements that we would consider to be theologically more important; and this is probably what often happens in such cases. Then in later years it is the non-rational element in the story that is recalled, and perhaps rejected at an age when the study of science in school is encouraging rationality. The result is often that the whole incident, or sometimes even the whole Bible, is then rejected.

It is not, of course, suggested that this is the result with all pupils who are taught by this method; still less that it will be the result with the boys in this school. Nor are we suggesting that the teaching given in this preparatory school had encouraged some of the boys to look at the biblical material in the way they did. Many other factors would need to be considered before we could venture an opinion on this matter.

Example 12 (pp. 44–5) illustrates the obvious fact that what is possible in one school is not necessarily possible in another. This large village county school has a good cross-section of children from working-class and middle-class homes, and the headteacher is a first-rate educationist. She knows the parents of all the children in her school, and she trains her teachers in the principles of primary-school education and puts at their disposal a library of teachers' books. There are some very bright children in the school and the general standard of work is high.

In such a situation some of the children can be stretched beyond what would normally be regarded as appropriate in a less favourable situation. Although the biblical material used in this team-teaching exercise might be considered to be too sophisticated for use in most junior schools, here it seemed to succeed with at least some of the brighter pupils.

More will be said about the use of the Bible in Chapter VI, which deals with the future of religious education in the primary school (pp. 63ff.).

INTEGRATION

Example 5 (pp. 41–2) illustrates a simple form of integration in the classroom. When the appearance of the apples was being enjoyed the lesson was an exercise in art appreciation; when the growth of a tree was discussed it became a science lesson; and the skilful way in which the story was told turned it into a literature lesson. All these elements were present, yet it was a truly integrated unity.

This was an aided Methodist school and it was therefore not inappropriate that in the closing moments of the lesson these junior children should experience a communion (eating together) and a Eucharist (thanksgiving) at a level which they could enjoy and at least partially understand.

TEAM TEACHING

Example 13 (p. 45) illustrates this method of teaching. The project was planned during the summer holiday and it was therefore teacher-guided rather than springing spontaneously from the children's suggestions. A good deal of Bible teaching was included in the exercise. For group work the children were divided into three teams, each of which tackled one of the subjects listed. When the project had been completed the teams came together and staged a joint exhibition of the work they had produced, and individual children described and explained their exhibits.

A feature of this kind of teaching is the considerable breadth of knowledge required to initiate and direct it. Such versatility is unlikely to be found in any one teacher, but it becomes possible when a team of teachers work together in this integrated way.

THEME TEACHING

It is difficult to comment on the individual examples of theme teaching described above (examples 7, 8, 9, 10, and 11, pp. 42–4). The subject is discussed at length elsewhere in this report (pp. 59–63), and the reader should return to these examples and look at them critically in the light of that discussion. When it has been studied.

ASSEMBLIES

This subject is also dealt with elsewhere (pp. 65–7), and it is suggested that the same procedure be adopted as is proposed above for theme teaching.

One assembly, however, requires a brief explanation here. It is example 19 (p. 47). This school was the centre of an alarming situation. The children came from West Indian, Greek and Turkish Cypriot, and other cultural backgrounds. The West Indians were either evangelical Baptists or Roman Catholics, and they quarrelled among themselves. Added to this there was antipathy between some of the white people in the neighbourhood and the coloured people, and a generally apathetic attitude to religion among the parents of many of the white children. The result of this situation was racial disharmony, bitter quarrels between the parents of children in the school, and even physical violence.

The nativity play at an assembly to which parents were invited was devised in a deliberate attempt to alleviate parental disharmony. The verdict of the headteacher was that the parents who saw it were so moved that quarrelling died down, and at the time of our visit, six months later, it had not broken out again.

VI. The way forward (CmJ)

1. The aims of religious education in the primary school

The kind of 'religious instruction' envisaged in the 1944 Education Act, and worked out in detail in the immediately post-war agreed syllabuses, failed to do what it set out to do: namely, in the words used in one of the syllabuses, 'to present the revelation of God given in the Bible' (*The West Riding Syllabus of Religious Instruction* (1947), Junior Section, p. 29). Most educationists are in any case now convinced that this aim is the wrong one. What, then, ought teachers to be trying to do in the primary schools of today? The first essential, if religious education is to become more effective, is that teachers should be clear about its real purpose. When that is decided it will be time to consider how to set about fulfilling that purpose.

There is uncertainty in the minds of many teachers today about the aims of religious education. The dichotomy in their thinking is between the educational aim of helping children to understand religion, and the evangelistic aim of helping to make children religious. Some still cling to the latter and are unwilling to accept the former wholeheartedly as the proper aim in county schools. The latter aim is, of course, appropriate in the home and in church, synagogue, temple, or mosque, but the former is the only legitimate aim in state schools when, in this secular age, they can no longer be thought of as Christian communities. The report, mentioned above (p. 22), of the working party appointed by the Social Morality Council speaks clearly on this subject:

> It is not the purpose of RE in the county school to bring about a commitment to the Christian faith, but rather to help children to understand what the Christian faith means in the context of other beliefs sincerely held by men and women of integrity and goodwill who do not find it possible to accept Christian commitment as the basis of their lives. (*Moral and Religious Education in County Schools*, p. 13)

A few teachers reject this point of view and say bluntly that they regard it as their duty to instil Christian beliefs into the children in their charge. Other teachers, by using religious words without explaining them, telling Bible stories uncritically, and engaging children in specifically Christian worship, are suggesting to children that they ought to adopt a particular point of view and accept one body of belief rather than another. In so doing they are acting as evangelists rather than teachers, and as missionaries rather than educators. They were appointed as teachers, and it is important that they should be faithful to their appointment and accept their role as educationists. Something has been said on this subject earlier in the report, in the chapter on recent trends in religious education (pp. 17ff.), and it should now be referred to again and reconsidered in the light of what is being said here about the way forward in the primary school.

The situation in a voluntary church school is in one sense the same as, and in another sense different from, the situation in a maintained school. It is the same in that children are subject to the same psychological principles, and they go through the same stages of mental development whether they attend a county school or a voluntary school. In both kinds of schools, therefore, the same educational considerations should be applied and the same teaching methods used. The situation in the two kinds of schools is somewhat different, however, in that the voluntary school may, and the county school may not, try to achieve its purpose 'through involvement in one particular religious tradition' (*The Fourth R*, para. 554). That this situation may have an important bearing on the kind of religious education given in a voluntary school cannot be doubted. Where there are Christian teachers in a church school which is closely linked to a truly worshipping community the children in such a school will be in a special kind of environment and, although they will have no special advantage in religious understanding over children in a county school, they will experience religion in its proper context of caring and love. Needless to say, teachers in county schools can exercise the same qualities of care and love as can teachers in church schools, and children in such county schools will then enjoy the experience that these qualities create.

In both kinds of schools, county and voluntary, the teaching should be open, in the sense that opinions are not forced upon children, who are free to question, to inquire, and to doubt. It should provide children with opportunities for exploring their own and other people's experience to enable them to discover what religion is about; so that whether they eventually accept or reject a religious way of life, they will at least know what it is they are accepting or rejecting.

2. Theme teaching

Goldman originally used the term 'life-theme' for what is now more usually called simply a theme, and in his book, *Readiness for Religion* (Routledge & Kegan Paul, 1965), he explains what he means by this term. 'A life-theme can

59

take any area of a child's life, of which he has first-hand knowledge. It should be about matters in which he has a natural interest and in which a large amount of diverse detail can be explored, related together in a meaningful unity and seen at a level of religious thinking within the capacities of the child.' A life-theme 'may begin with a religious emphasis or end with religion as a focal point', or it may have 'biblical illustration throughout' (p. 111). The intention is to help children eventually to reach an understanding of biblical imagery by enlarging their experience and improving their grasp of biblical metaphors. An example may bring out some of the possibilities in using Goldman's life-themes, and also point to some of the defects they contain.

In using the work-cards, *Shepherds and Sheep* compiled by Ronald Dingwell in the *Readiness for Religion* series (Rupert Hart-Davis, 1965), children of 7 and 8 years old are encouraged to find out about a sheep farm, sheep dipping and shearing, wool and its uses, shepherds in Palestine, etc. Goldman says that this kind of preliminary work is 'not wasted, but helps the child to see the "real" experience underlying the religious language he will hear later' (*Readiness for Religion*, p. 113). The last work-card deals with Jesus, the good shepherd, and the teacher's notes accompanying it say that it 'is designed to centre round a class or school act of worship' in which 'finally all say "thank you" through the prayer of one child addressed to God for Jesus being the Good Shepherd'. The defect in this is surely obvious, for Goldman's own research shows that this transference from concrete to abstract thinking is quite beyond the children of 7 and 8 for whom this life-theme is intended. In the light of Goldman's many examples of God–Jesus confusion in young children, this use of the theme would seem to make it doubly unsuitable. Furthermore, the idea of Jesus as the good shepherd cannot possibly spring spontaneously from the child's experience: it must be imposed by the teacher. The result is the very opposite of what was intended. This treatment can only serve to *separate* religion from life.

This kind of theme teaching represents the pioneering work that probably had to be done before its deficiencies could be recognized and a better kind could be evolved, and in that sense it has served a useful purpose. In practice, however, it has proved to be unsatisfactory both educationally and theologically, and if the quality of religious education in the primary schools is to improve it is essential that this kind of theme teaching should be abandoned without delay. Unfortunately, it is the only kind with which many teachers are familiar, and in schools where theme teaching is used in religious education it is more than likely that themes of this kind will be the ones in use. It is the more necessary, therefore, that teachers and headteachers should be familiar with another form of theme teaching which is theologically and educationally more valid than the earlier form, and an attempt must now be made to explain this other form.

An article by Jean Holm, 'Life-themes: what are they?' in *Learning for Living*, volume 9 (November 1969), gives a most useful account of thematic teaching and comes to grips with some of the theological issues involved. It is these theological issues that teachers must understand if they are to use themes effectively. Jean Holm makes a distinction between two kinds of themes: those which explore Bible imagery, and those which explore human experience. By means of Bible image themes children learn about the way of life in which the great biblical images such as shepherd, bread, water, etc., are rooted. Children still in the concrete stage of thinking will not grasp the full significance of the imagery, but they will find out a good deal about life in Bible times and how the Bible came to be written, all of which will contribute to the building up of an essential basis for later understanding. Themes of this kind are particularly appropriate at junior- and early secondary-school level; that is, at the concrete operational stage when children's curiosity is boundless and when they delight in fact-finding.

In using themes which explore human experience the starting-point is the child's own interest and his involvement in his immediate world. He is encouraged to explore his own experience and to learn from it. Discussion will play an important part in this exploration; discussion between the teacher and individual children or the teacher and small groups of children, as well as occasional class discussion. A teacher who is skilful at posing questions and helping children to savour experiences can do a great deal to heighten awareness and to encourage intellectual development.

With older pupils this kind of exploration can reach out to some of the profound questions of human existence, but where can the religious element be found in the experience of young children? In the traditional forms of religious education the 'religious' has usually been identified with teaching about God or Jesus, and with saying prayers and singing hymns. This concept greatly influenced early thinking about theme teaching, so that despite a unifying intention the actual result was that religion appeared as something apart from, and other than, real life. The religious elements in a theme exploring human experience with young children should be implicit in the experience itself. As Jean Holm says:

A religious interpretation of life does not mean bringing together and seeing the relationship between religion and life as though they were two separate spheres. It means being able to recognise and interpret religious values and

61

concepts even when they are not met in specifically 'religious' contexts or expressed in religious language.

Theological insights come to us through what is known in human experience. For example, we infer the being and the nature of God from what has been experienced in human life. Articulated inference and expression can only come when the formal operational stage of thinking has been reached at a mental age of about 13 years, but, to quote Jean Holm again, any experience, be it joyous or sad, 'which helps children to understand themselves and other people better, to understand better their relationship to other people and to the world, is laying the right foundation for later development of these basic theological concepts.'

Approaches to Religious Education: a Handbook of Suggestions (Hampshire LEA, 1970) and *Religious Education: Suggestions for Teachers* (Cambridge LEA, 1970) give many examples of thematic work based on these principles.

In the Albert Leavesley Memorial Lecture 1970, 'The theology of themes', John Hull gives a profound interpretation of the theology behind theme teaching. It is based upon the understanding of two subjects: the relationship between the sacred and the secular, and the concept of divine revelation. Thorough-going theme teaching of the kind envisaged in this section of our report assumes that religious experience is normal, everyday experience understood in depth, and not specific experience associated with special people, places, and objects said to be 'religious'. It is recognized that this distinction is a complex one and that 'educators urgently need help from philosophers of religion at this point' (p. 5). Of the two views, the one commonly held, and the one probably held by most teachers of religious education, is that religious experience is specific, whereas thematic teaching 'commits the teacher to the view that religious experience is not specific' (p. 6). Those teachers who believe that religious experience is restricted to specifically religious situations are the ones most likely to be worried because they see so little 'religion' in a theme, and they will try to drag into their teaching something which they consider to be definitely religious before the end of a theme is reached.

Similarly, most teachers of religious education probably believe, as probably do most Christians, that divine revelation is specific and restricted to special people and occasions, whereas thematic teaching in religious education assumes that revelation is also general as well as specific, and that people on all occasions are able to receive revelation. Teachers who do not accept this latter point of view, or who do not recognize that it is the basis on which themes in

62

religious education should be constructed, will obviously fail to see anything religious in such themes.

John Hull suggests that this kind of general revelation is not the only way, or even the most important way, in which God communicates with man. That is why themes in themselves are not sufficient in religious education. They may be adequate in the primary school, but, he goes on to say, Christian teaching 'must ultimately seek to interpret human experience not only in the light of the hopes and fears of men but in the light of the death and resurrection of Jesus Christ.' (p. 7)

We have urged the necessity of abandoning the kind of theme teaching which creates a false distinction between religion and life, between the sacred and the secular, and we must now press for its replacement by the more viable kind of theme teaching just explained. We recognize that this new kind of religious education requires in teachers a high degree of theological insight and educational expertise, but we press for it nevertheless. It would be wrong to do so, however, if we did not at the same time acknowledge that most teachers in primary schools will require further theological, and perhaps educational, training if they are to be equal to the demands of this method of teaching, and if we did not also suggest most forcibly that training of this kind should be made available as soon as possible for as many students and teachers as possible. The practical suggestions for the conduct of such a training programme are set out elsewhere in this report (pp. 69–70).

3. The use of the Bible

The thematic approach to religious education includes the use of Bible image themes (p. 61), and these call for teaching in which the aim is to introduce children to the background of the Bible. This is altogether appropriate material for teaching in the primary school where children are at the concrete stage of their development. Furthermore, it builds up a bank of factual information which can be drawn upon when the time comes, in the secondary school, to study the imagery underlying important biblical words like father, judge, servant, shepherd, bread, etc., in the light of their eastern biblical, and not their western modern, background.

Teaching of this kind covers a wide and fascinating field, and children should enjoy exploring it. The following topics are suitable at primary level: homes and families, school and games, sheep and shepherds, clothes and jewellery, wells and water, houses and furniture, corn and bread, trades and professions, learning and working, highways and journeys, Bible lands, the Bible library, the Bible translated into many languages, and how people have been influenced by the Bible.

Violet Madge, in her *Introducing Young Children to Jesus* (SCM Press, 1971), suggests another way in which the Bible may be used in primary schools. She shows how some of the stories in the gospels have significance for young children if they are allowed to spring naturally from shared experiences or events and if they are told in close conjunction with them. The number of suitable stories is small, but the following, among others, are quoted.

The stories of the lost coin and the lost sheep are suitable for telling when something precious to a child has been lost and then found again: a favourite kitten or a special bead from a broken necklace. Children know the desolation they feel on losing something and the joy they experience on finding it, and they will discover an echo of their own situation in the stories Jesus told (*Introducing Young Children to Jesus*, pp. 61–3). Early in their lives children discover the pain of disappointment when things go wrong, and an occasion when disappointment is experienced is an appropriate time to tell the story of Jesus receiving the little children following their disappointment on being turned away by the disciples (pp. 64–5). Being rejected by one's acquaintances and then being accepted by a special friend is a common experience among children, which is closely paralleled in the story in which Zacchaeus, the despised tax-collector, is befriended by Jesus (pp. 65–6).

These and other stories are dealt with at length in Violet Madge's book, showing how this method can be used with young children, and suggesting written and other expressive work that can usefully accompany the stories.

The new religious education requires teachers to consider very carefully their selection of material from the Bible. Goldman's verdict that teachers in the past have taught 'too much too soon' is justified; and his assertion that abstract religious thinking is not possible before a mental age of 13 or 14 suggests that some Bible stories are unsuitable for use in the primary school. Nevertheless, the rich field of Bible background is waiting to be explored (see above, p. 63) and this, together with the Bible stories that can legitimately be told, provides enough material to cause us to question Goldman's dictum that 'the Bible is not a children's book'. If he means that some versions of the Bible are not suitable to put into the hands of young children for their private reading, we must agree; but if he means that there is nothing in the Bible, or about the Bible, that is suitable teaching material for children, we must disagree. Nevertheless, if the quality of religious education in the primary school is to improve, some teachers must be much more discriminating in their use of the Bible, and they must

64

allow their choice of material to be governed by sound educational and theological principles rather than by their own preferences.

One way of ensuring that a Bible story is suitable for telling to a given group of children and that it will be effectively told is for the teacher to ask himself, before telling the story, the following questions:

a   Do I really understand the theological meaning of this story?
b   Can I convey to these children enough of the theological meaning of this story to avoid misunderstanding?
c   Is what I shall say, or shall not say, in telling this story likely to give a false or an unworthy view of God or of man to these children at this stage of their development?
d   Is there anything I shall say in telling this story that these children will need to unlearn at a later stage?

If there is any suspicion that the answer to questions **a** or **b** is 'No', or that the answer to questions **c** or **d** is 'Yes', it is time to think again about the suitability of the story or about the way of telling it.

A Source Book of the Bible for Teachers, edited by R. C. Walton (SCM Press, 1970), contains a wealth of information on the background of Bible stories and the ways of selecting and telling them.

4. Assemblies

Worship at the beginning of the school day was almost universal even before the 1944 Education Act made it compulsory. Because the Act says nothing about the content of this compulsory worship, assemblies in most schools continued after 1944 to have the same pattern as before: namely, a simplified and abbreviated form of church service, with hymns, prayers, Bible reading, and sometimes a short talk. It is reasonable to ask if young children are really capable of engaging with profit in worship of this kind.

The many definitions of worship (for example, 'Offering him who is worthy the honour that is due to him', 'Response to God who has first drawn near to us', etc.), the theological presuppositions of worship (that God exists, that he is transcendent, immanent, and omnipresent), and the practical implications of worship are extremely daunting even for an adult. It surely goes without saying that any activity involving abstract ideas of this kind must be regarded as intellectually unsuitable for children in the primary-school age range.

Considerations of this kind have prompted educationists to question the suitability for young children of liturgical worship of the traditional kind, even

65

when watered down, and have brought about in recent years a transformation in primary-school assemblies. Changes in assembly patterns have not proceeded as rapidly as the corresponding changes in classroom patterns, but a transformation has occurred, as a glance at the descriptions of assemblies elsewhere in this report will quickly confirm (pp. 45–7). Nevertheless, the uncertainty of aim so frequently found in other aspects of religious education is obvious also in many assemblies. Some headteachers and teachers think of assembly in a county primary school as a purely social occasion, with perhaps a dash of moral education thrown in, and others think of it as a full-scale act of Christian worship. We suggest, with some trepidation – for we know how unacceptable the idea will be to many people – that the time has come to resolve this ambivalence by giving up the notion that a county primary school assembly ought to be an act of Christian worship in the commonly accepted sense. Perhaps the presence in many school assemblies of children of other faiths – Muslims, Sikhs, and Hindus, for example – makes it undesirable in any case to hold a Chrstian act of worship in such schools.

If a county primary school assembly is not to take the form of a Christian act of worship, what form should it take?

First, it should be a school activity in its own right that is capable of being justified on educational grounds.

Secondly, assembly should be an enjoyable corporate experience in which there is a place for participation in movement, mime, drama, dancing, and procession, and in which there are exciting sounds to hear and interesting shapes and colours to see.

Thirdly, a primary-school assembly should be closely integrated with the life and work of the school and the neighbourhood. Topics for assembly may spring from a situation in the classroom, which may be explored at greater depth than would be possible elsewhere, or which may be considered here from a different point of view. A topic of this kind might be related in assembly to other aspects of the life of the school, or work done by one group of children might be displayed in assembly and explained to the rest of the school. Alternatively, the situation that provides a topic for assembly may come from outside the school in the life of the neighbourhood.

With this kind of integration, assembly becomes a vital part of the total activity of the school, and it is seen by the children to be relevant rather than something entirely different from every other school event.

If the kind of assembly thus envisaged cannot properly be called an act of worship in the traditional sense, it most certainly brings children to the verge of worship, to what John Hull calls the 'threshold' of worship ('Worship and

66

the curriculum', in the *Journal of Curriculum Studies*, volume 1 (November 1969), pp. 208 ff.). Assembly in the primary school can then be thought of as that part of the curriculum which prepares children for worship. It is a training ground in which the feelings, attitudes, and emotions are educated so that ultimately they will be based on truth rather than illusion, be governed by reason rather than caprice, and be directed to worthy rather than unworthy objects and ideas. To this end, situations must be created in assembly which will evoke from children responses such as the following: reverence in contemplating the supreme values of beauty, truth, and love; sympathy for deprived and otherwise unfortunate people; delight at being alive in the modern world; admiration for the human virtues of decency, honesty, self-sacrifice, courage, etc.; wonder in the presence of the marvels of the natural world; awe in the presence of majesty and mystery; anger at the sight of cruelty, injustice, exploitation, etc.; sorrow for human frailty and failure. Needless to say, the examples used in assembly will be specific and concrete and not, as the language used here might suggest, abstract in form.

If responses of this kind in their almost limitless variety are genuinely and deeply experienced by children in assembly they will be acquiring the basic presuppositions of worship, without which true worship is not possible. In true worship, as usually defined, the worshippers deliberately and consciously associate the exercise with thoughts about God. A primary-school assembly of the kind described above will not be an act of worship according to this definition, because most of the children will not associate it with thoughts about God.

5. Worship

In the light of what has been said about assemblies, has worship any relevance in the primary-school situation? We think it may be significant in two ways, although schools differ so considerably in circumstances and staffing that it is dangerous to generalize.

We have suggested earlier in this report (p. 65) that we think it impossible that young children are able to engage meaningfully in traditional forms of worship. This does not mean, however, that we think they cannot profitably share in the emotional experience of worship. We do not suggest that young children should themselves be asked to pray, or that adults should pray 'over' children. We recognize, nevertheless, that there may be significance for a child's religious education in a situation in which teachers who hold their religion as a living faith relevant to daily life occasionally say brief prayers in the presence of the children.

There must be no insistence that children should join in these prayers ('Hands together, eyes closed'), and they are better not said at all than said as a formality or 'for the sake of the children'. Their educational value does not lie in the words spoken, but in the felt atmosphere of worship, in the sensing that what is happening is of importance to adults whom the children respect and love. Primary-school children will not understand the full implications of prayer, but in this situation they will be sharing an emotional experience in the context of adult worship which in itself, although not conceptually acquired, is a valuable part of their education.

The singing by children and adults together of carefully chosen hymns and songs may be similarly regarded. The intellectual meaning of many words and phrases will escape children in the primary school, but the corporate nature of the activity, the pleasure of making melody in rhythm, and the sharing of an experience which the adults evidently enjoy and regard as important, may bring enrichment to the lives of the children and contribute something to their all-round development.

Worship is also relevant in the primary school in another way. Children may learn about the ways in which worship is practised by other people and in other faiths. There is an abundance of suitable material, and topics such as the following can be studied: buildings set apart for worship (ancient and modern churches, chapels, monasteries, synagogues, mosques, temples, shrines); sacred books used in worship (Bible, Torah, Koran); men and women devoted to worship (priests, ministers, monks, nuns); music used in worship (old and new hymns, psalms, church bells, organs, and other instruments); religious feasts and festivals, and their celebration (the Passover, the Lord's Supper, Ramadan); religious objects used in worship (altars, prayer shawls, phylacteries, prayer wheels, rosaries).

These topics should be dealt with at appropriate levels of understanding. Visual aids, including the actual objects where possible, and educational visits should play an important part in the study of them.

VII. Recommendations

1 A development project should be initiated as soon as possible to continue and expand the work begun by the present project.* Our survey suggests that the following are among the subjects in need of further investigation:

a the relationship between moral and religious education in the primary school;

b the place of prayer and worship in the primary school;

c the role of religious education in the middle years;

d the contribution to religious education of humanist and agnostic teachers in the primary school, and the relationship between the commitment of a teacher and the open approach to religious education;

e religious education for non-Christian immigrant children;

f the kinds of books, visual aids and other teaching materials required for use in religious education in the primary school.

2 Advisers in religious education and consultant teachers should be appointed in much greater number. A consultant teacher might work either with the staff of the school to which he or she is normally attached, or be released from duty – for one day a week, for instance – to visit other schools and offer help in religious education in an advisory capacity.

3 Students and teachers should be trained to meet the demands of the new religious education.

a In-service training courses for practising teachers should be provided in all parts of the country. The content of such courses and the best methods of conducting them are subjects needing further study. Method courses would in most cases be superfluous, and these are not generally recommended. Our observations prompt us to suggest that two kinds of courses are required: a course in the selection and interpretation of suitable biblical and non-biblical teaching material, including Bible background of the kind used in Bible image themes (p. 61); and a course dealing with the educational and theological presuppositions of the thematic approach to religious education. These courses could with advantage be shared by teachers in primary and secondary schools.

*See footnote to p. 5.

b   Courses of the kind recommended above for practising teachers should be included in all initial training courses.

c   Local seminars or workshops should be set up at which teachers overtaken by the revolution in religious education might discuss their problems with experts in this field. They should be ecumenical in composition and informal in style. Discussion, rather than lectures, should aim at dispelling the feeling of uncertainty and bewilderment that is so common among teachers of religious education today.

4   There should be more consultation between teachers of religious education in primary and secondary schools. This would most profitably be at local level, but conferences covering a wider area should occasionally be held. The new religious education at primary level is vastly different from the old. Many secondary-school teachers are unaware of the changes that have taken place, and many primary-school teachers are unaware of the ways in which religious education is developed in the secondary school. A meeting, say once or twice a term, of teachers in a group of associated schools would be extremely valuable in disseminating information and arranging agreed patterns of work.

5   Courses describing the needs of young children and the ways of meeting them, using modern methods of religious education, should be made available for clergy and ministers who teach or conduct assemblies in primary schools.

Appendices

Appendix A Questionnaire to nominated schools (J.C.)

Copy of the questionnaire completed by headteachers of the 213 nominated schools, omitting instructions and administrative details. More space was allowed for some answers than is given here.

A. SCHOOL

1. *Children*
   Number of **a** pupils on roll ....
                   b pupils withdrawn from religious education ....
                   c immigrant pupils **i** Christian ....
                                     ii non-Christian ....
   Please underline the age range of your pupils:
   5–7 / 5–9 / 8–11 / 8 or 9–13 / other
   If 'other', please state the age range ....

2. *Staff*
   Number **a** of teaching staff **i** part-time ....
                                  ii full-time ....
          b not taking part in religious education on conscientious grounds ....
          c who hold a college of education main course qualification in religious studies ....
          d who hold a further qualification in religious studies ....
                If **d**, please specify ....

3. *Environment*
   a Is the environment of the school mainly rural / urban / industrial / rural–urban? ....
   b Is the background of the pupils mainly working-class / middle-class / working- and middle-class in approximately equal numbers? ....

4. *Assembly*
   a In a typical week how many assemblies are
      i   for worship only   ....
      ii for notices and general school matters only   ....
      iii for worship and general school matters?   ....
   b In a typical week how many assemblies (excluding BBC services) are conducted mainly by

	infant	junior	combined
i the headteacher	....	....	....
ii the deputy-headteacher	....	....	....
iii assistant teacher	....	....	....
iv pupils	....	....	....
v visiting clergy	....	....	....
vi other visitors?	....	....	....

   c In a typical week how many assemblies for worship contain a story, movement or audio-visual section?   ....
   d Does your school use BBC religious services each week?   Yes / No
      If 'yes', on which day of the week
      Tuesday / Thursday / Friday?

5. *Curriculum*
   a Do classes work to a timetable for most school lessons?   Yes / No
   b Is religious education
      allocated timetable space / part of an integrated curriculum?
   c Are the classes in your school
      all streamed / all unstreamed / partly streamed / vertically grouped?
   d Does your school use some form of team teaching involving religious education?   Yes / No
   e Is expressive work, other than writing, used in religious education
      never / not very often because of organization difficulties / occasionally / as a general practice?
   f Which agreed syllabus is used in your school?
   ....

g How many copies of the agreed syllabus are there in the school? ....

h Do most of your staff use the agreed syllabus rarely / occasionally / often / very often / always?

i During the last school year did your school, or any part of it, carry out any community service?   Yes / No
If 'yes', please specify ....

j Is any attempt made to give moral education in your school
   i as part of a scheme of work apart from religious education   Yes / No
   ii as part of a religious education scheme?   Yes / No
     If 'yes' to either, please describe briefly the kind of thing you do
....

k Are you fairly satisfied with the present state of the moral education being given in your school?   Yes / No
Please give reasons for your answer
....

B. GENERAL

6. Which *two* of the following do you think have made the most significant contributions to current opinions on religious education
C. Alves / R. J. Goldman / K. G. Howkins / O. R. Johnston / R. S. Lee / V. Madge / H. F. Mathews / P. R. May / G. Moran / other?
If your choice is 'other', please specify ....

7. What in your opinion is the role of religious education in the life of your school
unimportant / not specially significant / no more important than any other school activity / highly significant / the most important item in the curriculum?

8. **a** Please give brief details of one or two examples of religious education work done since September 1969 that you consider to be especially interesting. Please name topic, type of activity, age of pupils, and class concerned
   i ....
   ii ....

b Will any of this work be available for us to see if we visit the school?   Yes / No

9. **a** Please give your own views on the aims of religious education

    ....

    b To what extent are you achieving these aims?

    ....

    c What do you need to help you to achieve these aims more effectively?

    ....

10. Please give your own views on the place of religion in school, religious education in general, or any other relevant subject

    ....

Appendix B   Questionnaire to schools in selected sub-sample

Copy of the questionnaire completed by teachers and headteachers of the fifty-six schools visited, omitting instructions and administrative details. This questionnaire was deliberately colloquial and friendly in tone, in the hope of gaining the teachers' ready co-operation.

1. In relation to the school's usual acts of worship, would you consider the *type* of assembly we've just seen to be –

    relatively unusual 1

    or   relatively usual 2

2. Thinking of this assembly again, on a 5-point scale, where would you say the degree of involvement in the assembly of *most* of the children would come? –

    completely immersed 1

    strongly interested... 2

    interested 3

    occasionally interested 4

    not interested... 5

3. **a**   Would you say *most* of your RE work is –

    not as enjoyable as most of your other work 1

    about the same as most of your other work 2

    more enjoyable than most of your other work 3

74

b Naturally, we shall be very interested in your response to the above question. Would you please say a little about the reasons for your response? ....
....

4. Please rate, in order of importance, 3 of the following factors that you consider present the greatest problems in your RE work –
  a fitting RE into the framework of the modern primary-school curriculum ....
  b your own personal biblical knowledge ....
  c the compulsory nature of religious education ....
  d your own religious beliefs..
  e the non-religious atmosphere of children's own home backgrounds ....
  f the lack of a class teacher with special knowledge of modern trends in RE, with responsibility for advising colleagues ....

5. Assuming the following cover the 2 most important groups of aims in RE, and you had to choose *just one* of them, please indicate which it would be,
  either, the group of RE aims most to do with the preparation for *ethical/humanitarian* development 1
  or, the group of RE aims most to do with *religious/spiritual* development 2

6. What specific RE work during the present year was the most successfully received? Please give **a** the content or title; **b** the method, activity, or materials used; and **c** how you judged it was successful.

7. Do you feel the compulsory teaching of RE –
  should be abolished 1
  should be retained 2

8. If compulsory RE were abolished, and you had the choice, would you decide to take part in –
  religious and moral education 1
  a form of moral education to be decided on an agreed basis 2
  neither religious nor moral education.................................. 3

9. If neither educational upset to children, nor inconvenience to your colleagues would result, would you prefer to opt out of RE work? Yes 1
  No 2

10. Is there anything in the way of *types* of books, *types* of visual aids, or anything that might help your RE in school that you feel should be developed as the subject of a later research study? ....

11. We'd be very grateful if you would underline the *one* category which most nearly describes your personal religious viewpoint—
atheist / nominal Christian / agnostic / committed Christian / humanist

Appendix C   Statistics

Table 1 Schools used in the survey

	COUNTY			VOLUNTARY						PREPARATORY
				Non-Catholic			Catholic			
	Infant	*Junior*	*JMI*	*Infant*	*Junior*	*JMI*	*Infant*	*Junior*	*JMI*	
Sample	44	53	39	7	10	46	5	2	5	2
Sub-sample visited	8	6	13	3	5	16	1	1	1	2

Table 2 Teachers with qualifications in religious studies

	Total number of teachers	Teachers with college of education qualification		Teachers with no college of education qualification		Teachers with other qualification		Teachers with no other qualification	
		No.	%	*No.*	%	*No.*	%	*No.*	%
Sample	2059	102	4·9	1957	95·1	76	3·6	1983	96·4
Sub-sample visited	538	36	6·7	502	93·3	13	2·4	525	97·6

The 'other qualification' most frequently named was the Archbishop's Certificate. Six teachers in the total sample had degree or diploma qualifications in religious studies.

Table 3 Teachers withdrawn from religious education

	Total number of teachers	Teachers withdrawn		Teachers not withdrawn	
		No.	%	*No.*	%
Sample	2059	32	1·6	2027	98·4
Sub-sample visited	538	15	2·8	523	97·2

Twelve (0·6 per cent) teachers withdrawn in the sample, and eight (1 5 per cent) teachers withdrawn in the sub-sample visited, were in schools having more than 3 per cent of the staff withdrawn.

Table 4 Personal beliefs of staff

Type of school	Staff	PERSONAL BELIEFS										Total
		Atheist		Agnostic		Humanist		Nominal Christian		Committed Christian		
		No.	%	No.	%	No.	%	No.	%	No.	%	
County	Headteachers	0	0	0	0	0	0	1	3·8	25	96·2	26
	Teachers	4	1·9	15	7·2	35	16·7	65	31·1	90	43·1	209
Voluntary Non-Catholic	Headteachers	0	0	0	0	0	0	2	9·5	19	90·5	21
	Teachers	0	0	4	2·7	15	10·3	36	24·7	91	62·3	146
Voluntary Catholic	Headteachers	0	0	0	0	0	0	0	0	3	100	3
	Teachers	0	0	0	0	0	0	1	5·0	19	95·0	20
Total for all schools	Headteachers	0	0	0	0	0	0	3	6·0	47	94·0	50
	Teachers	4	1·1	19	5·1	50	13·3	102	27·2	200	53·3	375

Table 5 Schools in which children are withdrawn from religious education

	Total number of schools	Schools in which children are withdrawn		10·0–5·0% withdrawn		4·9–1·0% withdrawn		Less than 1% withdrawn		None withdrawn	
		No.	%	No.	%	No.	%	No.	%	No.	%
Sample	213	70	32·9	4	1·9	21	9·9	45	21·1	143	67·1
Sub-sample visited	56	17	30·4	0	0	5	8·9	12	21·4	39	69·6

Table 6 Children withdrawn from religious education

	Total number of children on roll	Children withdrawn	
		No.	%
Sample	56 254	349	0·6
Sub-sample visited	14 283	39	0·3

Table 7 Schools in which there are non-Christian immigrant children

	Total number of schools	Schools with immigrant children		Schools with non-Christian immigrant children		More than 10% of roll		9·9–5·0% of roll		4·9–0·1% of roll		None	
		No.	%	No.	%	No.	%	No.	%	No.	%	No.	%
Sample	213	73	34·3	35	16·4	7	3·3	5	2·3	23	10·8	140	65·7
Sub-sample visited	56	23	41·1	12	21·4	3	5·4	2	3·6	7	12·5	33	58·9

Table 8 Schools in which there are Christian immigrant children

	Total number of schools	Schools with immigrant children		Schools with Christian immigrant children		More than 10% of roll		9·9–5·0% of roll		4·9–0·1% of roll		None	
		No.	%	No.	%	No.	%	No.	%	No.	%	No.	%
Sample	213	73	34·3	61	28·6	10	4·7	7	3·3	44	20·7	140	65·7
Sub-sample visited	56	23	41·1	18	32·1	3	5·4	2	3·6	13	23·2	33	58·9

Twenty-three schools in the sample, and seven schools in the sub-sample visited, have both non-Christian and Christian immigrant children.

Table 9 Immigrant children in schools

	Total number of children on roll	TOTAL NUMBER OF IMMIGRANT CHILDREN				Total number of non-immigrant children	
		Non-Christian		Christian			
		No.	%	No.	%	No.	%
Sample	56 254	721	1·3	989	1·8	54 544	97·0
Sub-sample visited	14 283	230	1·6	237	1·7	13 816	96·7

Bibliography

Approaches to Religious Education: a Handbook of Suggestions. Hampshire Education Committee, 1970.

COX, E. *Changing Aims in Religious Education.* Routledge & Kegan Paul, 1966.

DEAN, J. *Religious Education for Children.* Ward Lock, 1971.

The Fourth R: the Durham Report on Religious Education. National Society and SPCK, 1970.

GOLDMAN, R. J. *Religious Thinking from Childhood to Adolescence.* Routledge & Kegan Paul, 1964.

GOLDMAN, R. J. *Readiness for Religion.* Routledge & Kegan Paul, 1965.

KAY, W. *Moral Development.* Allen & Unwin, 1968.

Learning for Living, Volume 10, No. 3. January 1971. (Special issue devoted to religious education in the primary school, obtainable from Christian Education Movement, Annandale, North End Road, London NW 11)

LEE, R. S. *Your Growing Child and Religion* (Pelican). Penguin Books, 1965.

MADGE, V. *Children in Search of Meaning.* SCM Press, 1965.

MADGE, V. *Introducing Young Children to Jesus.* SCM Press, 1971.

MATHEWS, H. F. *Revolution in Religious Education.* Religious Education Press, 1966.

MATHEWS, H. F. *The New Religious Education.* Religious Education Press, 1971.

Moral and Religious Education in County Schools. Social Morality Council, 1970.

MORAN, G. *God Still Speaks.* Burns & Oates, 1967.

Religious Education: Suggestions for Teachers. Cambridgeshire and Isle of Ely Education Committee, 1970.

WALTON, R. C. (ed.) *A Source Book of the Bible for Teachers.* SCM Press, 1970.